P9-DFZ-950

Ecology
Experiments

FACTS ON FILE SCIENCE EXPERIMENTS

Ecology Experiments

Pamela Walker
Elaine Wood

Facts On File
An imprint of Infobase Publishing

Ecology Experiments

Facts On File, Inc.
An imprint of Infobase Publishing
132 West 31st Street
New York NY 10001

Library of Congress Cataloging-in-Publication Data
Walker, Pamela.
Ecology experiments / Pamela Walker, Elaine Wood.
p. cm.—(Facts on file science experiments)
Includes bibliographical references and index.
ISBN 978-0-8160-8169-1
1. Ecology–Experiments–Juvenile literature. 2. Science projects–Juvenile literature.
I. Wood, Elaine, 1950- II. Title.
QH541.14.W352010
577.072'4–dc22
2009051741

Facts On File books are available at special discounts when purchased in bulk quantities for businesses, associations, institutions, or sales promotions. Please call our Special Sales Department in New York at (212) 967-8800 or (800) 322-8755.

You can find Facts On File on the World Wide Web at http://www.factsonfile.com

All links and Web addresses were checked and verified to be correct at the time of publication. Because of the dynamic nature of the Web, some addresses and links may have changed since publication and may no longer be valid.

Editor: Frank K. Darmstadt
Copy Editor: Betsy Feist at A Good Thing, Inc.
Project Coordinator: Aaron Richman
Art Director: Howard Petlack
Production: Victoria Kessler
Illustrations: Hadel Studios
Cover printed by: Bang Printing, Brainerd, MN
Book printed and bound by Bang Printing, Brainerd, MN
Date printed: July 2010
Printed in the United States of America

10 9 8 7 6 5 4 3 2 1

This book is printed on acid-free paper.

Contents

Preface

For centuries, humans have studied and explored the natural world around them. The ever-growing body of knowledge resulting from these efforts is science. Information gained through science is passed from one generation to the next through an array of educational programs. One of the primary goals of every science education program is to help young people develop critical-thinking and problem-solving skills that they can use throughout their lives.

Science education is unique in academics in that it not only conveys facts and skills; it also cultivates curiosity and creativity. For this reason, science is an active process that cannot be fully conveyed by passive teaching techniques. The question for educators has always been, "What is the best way to teach science?" There is no simple answer to this question, but studies in education provide useful insights.

Research indicates that students need to be actively involved in science, learning it through experience. Science students are encouraged to go far beyond the textbook and to ask questions, consider novel ideas, form their own predictions, develop experiments or procedures, collect information, record results, analyze findings, and use a variety of resources to expand knowledge. In other words, students cannot just hear science; they must also do science.

"Doing" science means performing experiments. In the science curriculum, experiments play a number of educational roles. In some cases, hands-on activities serve as hooks to engage students and introduce new topics. For example, a discrepant event used as an introductory experiment encourages questions and inspires students to seek the answers behind their findings. Classroom investigations can also help expand information that was previously introduced or cement new knowledge. According to neuroscience, experiments and other types of hands-on learning help transfer new learning from short-term into long-term memory.

Facts On File Science Experiments is a twelve-volume set of experiments that helps engage students and enable them to "do" science. The high-interest experiments in these books put students' minds into gear and give them opportunities to become involved, to think independently, and to build on their own base of science knowledge.

As a resource, Facts On File Science Experiments provides teachers with new and innovative classroom investigations that are presented in a clear, easy-to-understand style. The areas of study in the six-volume set include forensic science, environmental science, computer research, physical science, weather and climate, and space and astronomy. Experiments are supported by colorful figures and line illustrations that help hold students' attention and explain information. All of the experiments in these books use multiple science process skills such as observing, measuring, classifying, analyzing, and predicting. In addition, some of the experiments require students to practice inquiry science by setting up and carrying out their own open-ended experiments.

Each volume of the set contains 20 new experiments as well as extensive safety guidelines, glossary, correlation to the National Science Education Standards, scope and sequence, and an annotated list of Internet resources. An introduction that presents background information begins each investigation to provide an overview of the topic. Every experiment also includes relevant specific safety tips along with materials list, procedure, analysis questions, explanation of the experiment, connections to real life, and an annotated further reading section for extended research.

Pam Walker and Elaine Wood, the authors of Facts On File Science Experiments, are sensitive to the needs of both science teachers and students. The writing team has more than 40 years of combined science teaching experience. Both are actively involved in planning and improving science curricula in their home state, Georgia, where Pam was the 2007 Teacher of the Year. Walker and Wood are master teachers who hold specialist degrees in science and science education. They are the authors of dozens of books for middle and high school science teachers and students.

Facts On File Science Experiments, by Walker and Wood, facilitates science instruction by making it easy for teachers to incorporate experimentation. During experiments, students reap benefits that are not available in other types of instruction. One of these benefits is the opportunity to take advantage of the learning provided by social interactions. Experiments are usually carried out in small groups, enabling students to brainstorm and learn from each other. The validity of group work as an effective learning tool is supported by research in neuroscience, which shows that the brain is a social organ and that communication and collaboration are activities that naturally enhance learning.

Experimentation addresses many different types of learning, including lateral thinking, multiple intelligences, and constructivism. In lateral thinking, students solve problems using nontraditional methods. Long-established, rigid procedures for problem-solving are replaced by original ideas from students. When encouraged to think laterally, students are more likely to come up with unique ideas that are not usually found in the traditional classroom. This type of thinking requires students to construct meaning from an activity and to think like scientists.

Another benefit of experimentation is that it accommodates students' multiple intelligences. According to the theory of multiple intelligences, students possess many different aptitudes, but in varying degrees. Some of these forms of intelligence include linguistic, musical, logical-mathematical, spatial, kinesthetic, intrapersonal, and interpersonal. Learning is more likely to be acquired and retained when more than one sense is involved. During an experiment, students of all intellectual types find roles in which they can excel.

Students in the science classroom become involved in active learning, constructing new ideas based on their current knowledge and their experimental findings. The constructivist theory of learning encourages students to discover principles for and by themselves. Through problem solving and independent thinking, students build on what they know, moving forward in a manner that makes learning real and lasting.

Active, experimental learning makes connections between newly acquired information and the real world, a world that includes jobs. In the twenty-first century, employers expect their employees to identify and solve problems for themselves. Therefore, today's students, workers of the near future, will be required to use higher-level thinking skills. Experience with science experiments provides potential workers with the ability and confidence to be problem solvers.

The goal of Walker and Wood in this multivolume set is to provide experiments that hook and hold the interest of students, teach basic concepts of science, and help students develop their critical-thinking skills. When fully immersed in an experiment, students can experience those "Aha!" moments, the special times when new information merges with what is already known and understanding breaks through. On these occasions, real and lasting learning takes place. The authors hope that this set of books helps bring more "Aha" moments into every science class.

Acknowledgments

This book would not exist were it not for our editor, Frank K. Darmstadt, who conceived and directed the project. Frank supervised the material closely, editing and making invaluable comments along the way. Betsy Feist of A Good Thing, Inc., is responsible for transforming our raw material into a polished and grammatically correct manuscript that makes us proud.

Introduction

Even though we spend much time inside our homes, schools, and offices, we are dependent on the natural world around us. Ecology is the study of that world, focusing on the interactions of living things with their environment and the transfer of energy through the system. The study of ecology helps the curious understand how the world around them operates. As an interdisciplinary science, it touches on many fields including genetics, atmospheric science, geology, chemistry, physiology, and hydrology.

Because the natural world has been here so much longer than the human race, we can learn a lot from studying it. Natural systems are balanced, healthy, and long-lived. The activities of humans are upsetting the complex, natural stability of organisms and energy in ecosystems, tipping the scale. An understanding of ecology can help us reestablish the equilibrium needed for long-term sustainability.

In classrooms, students learn ecology through discussion, lecture, and laboratory exercises. Experiments are especially useful learning strategies because they are hands-on activities that require and maintain student engagement. *Ecology Experiments* is one volume of the Facts On File Science Experiments set. The goal of this volume is to provide science teachers with 20 original experiments that convey basic principles related to ecology. The experiments in *Ecology Experiments* are proven classroom activities that broaden understandings of both ecological facts and the nature of science. The content of this volume is based on the three broad areas of the field of ecology: energy flow, recycling of nutrients, and populations.

Designed for both middle and high school classes, the book provides both indoor and outdoor activities. Experiments are presented in ways that help teachers accommodate a number of learning styles. Several of the lessons in *Ecology Experiments* are inquiries, experiments in which students are given a problem and asked to write a hypothesis, design and conduct an experiment, and draw conclusions. All of these inquiry experiments also serve as differentiation tools for teachers who want to fine-tune their instruction to individual students. Several experiments could be long-term projects that students work on part time. Experiments that provide students with the opportunities to carry out inquiries include "Diversity in Soil Ecosystems," which focuses on how the availability of water and nutrients and the condition of the soil affects soil ecosystems; "Surface Area Affects Body Temperature," an exercise in which students design experiments to find out how adaptations of body size and weight affect the metabolic rate and temperature of animals; "Energy in Ecosystems," in which students determine the effect of plant cover on ecosystem temperatures; and "The Role of Decomposers in the Nitrogen Cycle," an experiment to find out how nitrogen from decomposed leaves affects plant growth.

Because differentiated instruction is a key element in successful teaching, other experiments in the book provide differentiation opportunities. In "Biome Learning Centers," students or groups of students carry out research on one biome, create learning centers or lab stations on the biome, then share the stations with other students. This type of activity can be a long-term project that students work on for several weeks. Teachers can further differentiate by having students generate different products, with the faster students visiting all of the learning centers and the slower students visiting only a few.

The majority of experiments are presented in the traditional style in which students are given instructions to follow. The dynamics of populations and communities are the focus of four of these experiments. In "Size or Age Distributions in Populations," students study two types of trees in a community and find out how age structure affects population growth. "Species Diversity," an experiment that can be done indoors or outdoors, has students analyze the importance of diversity in a community. Students use cards to play the roles of lynx and hares in "Predator and Prey Populations." To learn about freshwater communities, students gather specimens in "Identifying the Benthos Community."

Experiments that feature the characteristics of ecosystems include "Monitoring Vegetative Cover," an activity that demonstrates the methods used by population biologists to keep an eye on changes in ecosystems. "Leaf Area Affects Primary Productivity" introduces the concepts of gross and net productivity and reinforces the concepts of photosynthesis and cellular respiration. "Food Webs" explains how energy flows through ecosystems. Students find out how the introduction of rabbits upset the Australian ecosystem in "Invasive Species' Impacts on an Ecosystem." Direct, outdoor observation helps students determine feeding relationships in "Components of an Ecosystem."

The unique characteristics of individual biomes are examined in "Observing Plant Growth in Different Biomes," an experiment that has students grow seedlings under different climatic conditions. In "Water Affects Temperatures in Biomes," students experimentally compare the abilities of water and soil to hold and retain heat. Changes in biomes are discussed in "What Are the Stages of Ecological Succession?" This experiment has students observe different stages of succession on the school campus. "Community Succession in Milk" shows how populations in a community changes as the environment changes. Adaptations of organisms to their biome are studied in "Day-Length Adaptations in Seeds," in which students determine whether or not day length affects rate of seed germination and in "How Effective Is Mimicry?" an experiment that simulates the survival rate of mimics and their models.

Students who spend some of their leisure time outdoors tend to be more familiar with the characteristics and problems of ecosystems than those who have limited outdoor opportunities. In some school systems, stepping outdoors is an easy option, yet in others it is impossible. Nevertheless, every science curriculum includes standards in ecology simply because Earth's citizens must understand our ecosystems to help keep them in balance.

The goals of sound ecology curricula include helping students understand how their local ecosystems work, as well as their own connections to more distant parts of the planet's biosphere. In this sense, the study of ecology can increase the awareness and sensitivity of students to their surroundings, helping them understand that the biosphere is thin and fragile. Students who recognize that each person has an impact on the biosphere are poised to live responsibly on the Earth.

Walker and Wood hope that instructors can use *Ecology Experiments* to aid students in perceiving themselves and their immediate surrounding as part of interconnected world community. Teachers can give students new eyes for seeing the roles and relationships of all organisms, from fungi in the tropics to plankton in the Arctic. By enabling students to reason through and solve ecological problems in the classroom, teachers empower them to solve similar problems in the real world.

Safety Precautions

REVIEW BEFORE STARTING ANY EXPERIMENT

Each experiment includes special safety precautions that are relevant to that particular project. These do not include all the basic safety precautions that are necessary whenever you are working on a scientific experiment. For this reason, it is absolutely necessary that you read and remain mindful of the General Safety Precautions that follow. Experimental science can be dangerous and good laboratory procedure always includes following basic safety rules. Things can happen quickly while you are performing an experiment—for example, materials can spill, break, or even catch on fire. There will not be time after the fact to protect yourself. Always prepare for unexpected dangers by following the basic safety guidelines during the entire experiment, whether or not something seems dangerous to you at a given moment.

We have been quite sparing in prescribing safety precautions for the individual experiments. For one reason, we want you to take very seriously the safety precautions that are printed in this book. If you see it written here, you can be sure that it is here because it is absolutely critical.

Read the safety precautions here and at the beginning of each experiment before performing each lab activity. It is difficult to remember a long set of general rules. By rereading these general precautions every time you set up an experiment, you will be reminding yourself that lab safety is critically important. In addition, use your good judgment and pay close attention when performing potentially dangerous procedures. Just because the book does not say "Be careful with hot liquids" or "Don't cut yourself with a knife" does not mean that you can be careless when boiling water or using a knife to punch holes in plastic bottles. Notes in the text are special precautions to which you must pay special attention.

GENERAL SAFETY PRECAUTIONS

Accidents can be caused by carelessness, haste, or insufficient knowledge. By practicing safety procedures and being alert while conducting experiments, you can avoid taking an unnecessary risk. Be sure to check the individual experiments in this book for additional safety regulations and adult supervision requirements. If you will be working in a laboratory, do not work alone. When you are working off site, keep in groups with a minimum of three students per group, and follow school rules and state legal requirements for the number of supervisors required. Ask an adult supervisor with basic training in first aid to carry a small first-aid kit. Make sure everyone knows where this person will be during the experiment.

PREPARING

- Clear all surfaces before beginning experiments.
- Read the entire experiment before you start.
- Know the hazards of the experiments and anticipate dangers.

PROTECTING YOURSELF

- Follow the directions step by step.
- Perform only one experiment at a time.
- Locate exits, fire blanket and extinguisher, master gas and electricity shut-offs, eyewash, and first-aid kit.
- Make sure there is adequate ventilation.
- Do not participate in horseplay.
- Do not wear open-toed shoes.
- Keep floor and workspace neat, clean, and dry.
- Clean up spills immediately.
- If glassware breaks, do not clean it up by yourself; ask for teacher assistance.
- Tie back long hair.
- Never eat, drink, or smoke in the laboratory or workspace.
- Do not eat or drink any substances tested unless expressly permitted to do so by a knowledgeable adult.

USING EQUIPMENT WITH CARE

- Set up apparatus far from the edge of the desk.
- Use knives or other sharp, pointed instruments with care.

- Pull plugs, not cords, when removing electrical plugs.
- Clean glassware before and after use.
- Check glassware for scratches, cracks, and sharp edges.
- Let your teacher know about broken glassware immediately.
- Do not use reflected sunlight to illuminate your microscope.
- Do not touch metal conductors.
- Take care when working with any form of electricity.
- Use alcohol-filled thermometers, not mercury-filled thermometers.

USING CHEMICALS

- Never taste or inhale chemicals.
- Label all bottles and apparatus containing chemicals.
- Read labels carefully.
- Avoid chemical contact with skin and eyes (wear safety glasses or goggles, lab apron, and gloves).
- Do not touch chemical solutions.
- Wash hands before and after using solutions.
- Wipe up spills thoroughly.

HEATING SUBSTANCES

- Wear safety glasses or goggles, apron, and gloves when heating materials.
- Keep your face away from test tubes and beakers.
- When heating substances in a test tube, avoid pointing the top of the test tube toward other people.
- Use test tubes, beakers, and other glassware made of Pyrex™ glass.
- Never leave apparatus unattended.
- Use safety tongs and heat-resistant gloves.
- If your laboratory does not have heatproof workbenches, put your Bunsen burner on a heatproof mat before lighting it.
- Take care when lighting your Bunsen burner; light it with the airhole closed and use a Bunsen burner lighter rather than wooden matches.

- Turn off hot plates, Bunsen burners, and gas when you are done.
- Keep flammable substances away from flames and other sources of heat.
- Have a fire extinguisher on hand.

FINISHING UP

- Thoroughly clean your work area and any glassware used.
- Wash your hands.
- Be careful not to return chemicals or contaminated reagents to the wrong containers.
- Do not dispose of materials in the sink unless instructed to do so.
- Clean up all residues and put in proper containers for disposal.
- Dispose of all chemicals according to all local, state, and federal laws.

BE SAFETY CONSCIOUS AT ALL TIMES!

1. Size or Age Distributions in Populations

Topic

The size or age distribution of a population provides information about the population's viability.

Introduction

Three aspects of any population are density, distribution, and age structure. Density, which refers to the number of individuals in a given area, affects the ability of individuals to find the space, food, and water they need for survival. The distribution of a population describes where organisms are positioned throughout the given area. In some habitats, resources are evenly distributed, so organisms may be uniformly spread throughout the space. In other habitats, resources are clustered in certain areas and so are the inhabitants. Age structure of a population refers to the relative number of individuals in each age group.

Depending on the population, age structure can be examined in different ways. For example, in the human population, age structure can be analyzed by determining the age of each individual in years and months. In insects, age is measured by life stage, such as egg, larva, pupa, or adult (see Figure 1). In some plants, age can be estimated by height or diameter while in others it can be found by counting rings. In this experiment, you will determine and analyze age structures of tree populations.

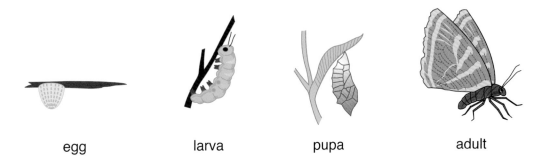

egg   larva   pupa   adult

Figure 1

Life stages of a butterfly

Time Required

45 minutes for part A
45 minutes for part B

Materials

- ◦◦ graph paper
- ◦◦ green pencil
- ◦◦ brown pencil
- ◦◦ tape measure
- ◦◦ hand lens
- ◦◦ science notebook

Safety Note   Please review and follow the safety guidelines at the beginning of this volume.

Procedure, Part A

1. Figure 2 shows cross sections of pines and oak trees in a forest. Pine trees are green and oak trees are brown. Use a hand lens to help you count the number of rings in each pine tree and record the data in your science notebook.

2. Use the hand lens to count the number of rings in each oak tree and record the data in your science notebook.

3. Copy the Data Table 1 in your science notebook. Use the counts of rings in pines and oak from steps 1 and 2 to complete it. You will need to extend the table to accommodate the data.

4. Use the data to create a graph showing the age structures of the pine tree population and the oak tree population. Use the green pencil to show pines and the brown pencil to show oaks.

5. Answer Analysis questions 1 through 3.

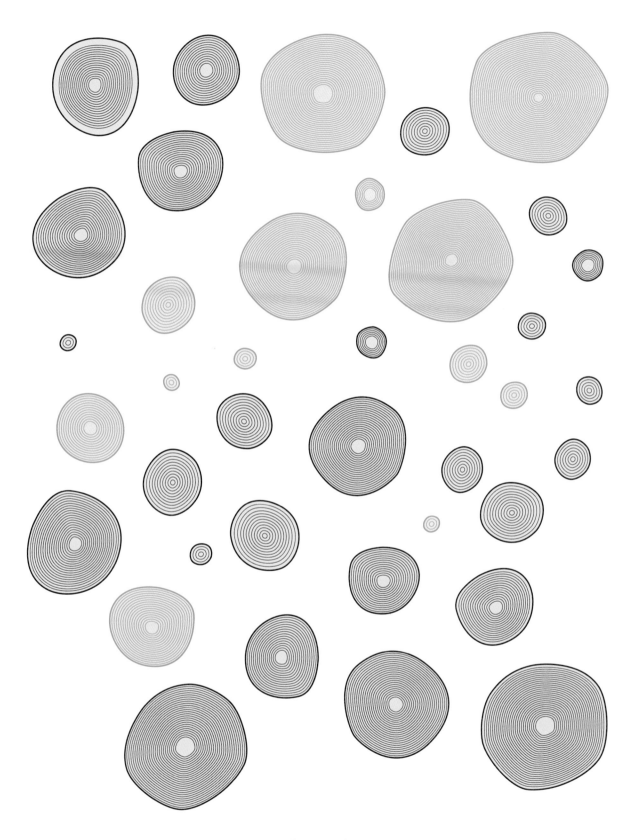

Figure 2

Data Table 1

Number of rings	Pines	Oaks
3		
4		
5		
6		
7		
8		
9		
10		

Procedure, Part B

1. Follow your teacher to an outdoor area where there is a population of trees.

2. Working with a partner, select one type of tree to measure. You might select pines, oaks, or any other type of tree that grows in your area.

3. Measure each of the trees of the type you selected within the outdoor area. To carry out your measurement, determine the diameter of the tree at breast height (dbh).

4. Create a data table in your science notebook to record the data.

5. When you return to the science classroom, create a graph based on your data.

6. Answer Analysis questions 4 through 6.

Analysis

1. Based on your graph in part A, which is the youngest population, oaks or pines? Explain your reasoning.

2. Which of the populations is faster growing, oaks or pines? Explain your reasoning.

3. What are some disadvantages of determining the ages of trees by counting rings?

4. Based on your outdoor findings, would you describe the population of trees you measured as young, middle aged, or mature? Explain your reasoning.

5. What are some disadvantages of determining the ages of trees using the dbh method?

6. Data Tables 2 and 3 below show two populations of palm trees, one on a golf course and one in a natural area. In this study, ecologists measured the height of the trees to determine age. Answer the following questions about the graphs:

   a. Which graph represents the golf course? How do you know?

   b. Which graph represents an area where young trees are growing and maturing?

   c. Which graph represents an area where there will be few trees to replace the mature ones when they die?

Data Table 2

Percentage of population		0	5	10	15	20	25	30
	70							
	60					▓		
	50					▓	▓	
	40					▓	▓	
	30					▓	▓	
	20					▓	▓	▓
	10					▓	▓	▓

Stem height in meters (m)

Data Table 3

Percentage of population	70							
	60							
	50							
	40							
	30							
	20							
	10							
		0	5	10	15	20	25	30

Stem height in meters (m)

What's Going On?

Understanding the age structure can help one understand the growth of a population. In populations that have high proportions of individuals in preproductive or reproductive stages, the potential for growth is high. Populations made up primarily of older individuals will show very little growth. In part A of this experiment, you counted rings of two populations of trees. The oaks are a very young population with a high proportion of young individuals to adults. As a result, this population is viable and will be producing young trees for a long time. The pines are a older population with a smaller proportion of young to mature trees. Older populations are at risk of dying out.

Animal populations can be analyzed using techniques similar to those in this experiment. The ages of populations can be represented with age pyramids, with proportions of individuals in each group shown. Younger individuals are at the bottom of the pyramid and older ones at the top. For example, an opossum population is 75 percent young and 25 percent adults. This 3:1 ratio indicates a fast growing group. A deer population has 60 percent young and 40 percent adult, a stable population structure that shows normal growth. An endangered owl population has 20 percent young and 80 percent adult, indicating no growth. There will not be enough young owls coming along to replace the old owls when they die, and the population will shrink.

Connections

Before 1750, human population growth rate was slow. Growth rate is a percentage that reflects the difference in the number of births and deaths each year. After 1750, worldwide growth rate increased, peaking at 2 percent in 1965. Today, more-developed countries (MDC) like Europe and North America have shown a slowdown in growth rate. Less-developed countries (LDC), including India, Asia, and Africa, still have fast growth. The growth structure pyramids shown in Figure 3 indicate this difference.

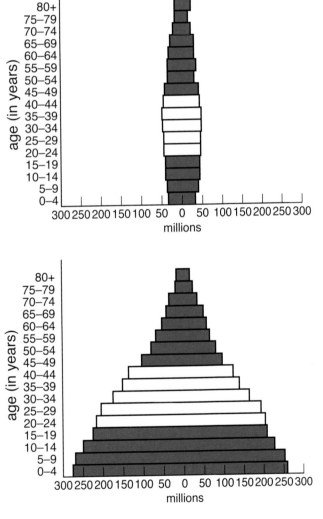

Figure 3

Growth structure pyramids of more-developed countries (MDC) and less-developed countries (LDC)

The pyramids show that in MDC, most of the population is made up of adults. This type of pyramid indicates a stable population in which there will be little growth. In LDC, the bottom of the pyramid is wide, indicating that a large percentage of the population is made up of people who are younger than 15 years. Even if each of these individuals has fewer children than his or her parents, the population will continue to grow.

Want to Know More?

See appendix for Our Findings.

Further Reading

Cobb, Loren. "Population Dynamics," February 13, 2005. Available online. URL: http://www.aetheling.com/NL/sim/population/population1.html. Accessed July, 23, 2009. This simulation shows how changes in fertility, infant mortality, and other parameters affect changes in population dynamics.

National Park Service. "Dall Sheep Population Size." Available online. URL: http://www.nps.gov/akso/parkwise/Students/ReferenceLibrary/WEAR/DallSheepPopulation.htm. Accessed July 23, 2009. The National Park Services uses dall sheep to explain the dynamics of populations.

Sharov, Alexei. "Quantitative Population Ecology." Department of Entomology, Virginia Tech. Available online. URL: http://home.comcast.net/~sharov/PopEcol/. Accessed July 22, 2009. Dr. Sharov's lectures on population ecology, which are appropriate for the advanced student, are available on this Web site.

2. Species Diversity

Topic

A natural community contains a wide diversity of species.

Introduction

A *community* is a group of individuals of different species, each with its own *niche* or way of using available resources to sustain itself. The species that live in a community are those that can survive in the environmental conditions. Only a limited number of species are adapted to each unique set of circumstances that a community can offer. For this reason, patterns of similar groups of species recur in communities with similar characteristics.

The richness of species in a community is referred to as *biodiversity*, the variety of life-forms. No one knows for sure how many species of organisms inhabit Earth. The most common living things are very small and difficult to quantify. Scientists estimate that there are 5 to 30 million different kinds of organisms alive—less than 2 million have been identified and named. In this experiment, you will calculate biodiversity and analyze your calculations.

Time Required

30 minutes for part A
45 minutes for part B

Materials

- access to an outdoor area
- science notebook

| Safety Note | Please review and follow the safety guidelines at the beginning of this volume. |

Procedure, Part A

1. Copy the data table in your science notebook twice, calling them Data Table 1 and Data Table 2.

2. Examine Figure 1 (below), which shows a community that supports six species of animals. Count the number of each species and record that number on Data Table 1.

3. Examine Figure 2, which shows a community that also supports six species of animals. Count the number of each species and record that number on Data Table 2.

4. Calculate the biodiversity of each community. To do so, use the following formula:

$$\text{biodiversity index} = \frac{\text{number of species in the area}}{\text{total number of individuals in the area}}$$

5. Answer Analysis questions 1 through 4.

Figure 1

Community A

Figure 2

Community B

Procedure, Part B

1. Follow your teacher to an outdoor area. The area you will be assigned represents a community.

2. Copy the data table in your science notebook. You will probably need to extend the length of the table.

3. Count the number of species in your assigned area and the number of individuals within each species. If you do not know the name of a species, ask your teacher or simply give it a name such as "species A" or "species B."

4. Determine the biodiversity index of the community you examined.

5. When you return to the classroom, share your findings with other students.

6. Answer Analysis questions 5 through 7.

Analysis

1. In your own words, define *biodiversity*.

2. Which community (Figure 1 or Figure 2) contains the most biodiversity?

Data Table	
Species	**Number of individuals of this species**

3. Calculate the biodiversity index for a plot that has 40 earthworms, but no other species.

4. Calculate the biodiversity index for a plot that has three earthworms, 3 crickets, four centipedes, five grasshoppers, five millipedes, four sow bugs, two moles, two ferns, three filamentous fungi, and nine ants.

5. What was the biodiversity index of the outdoor area you analyzed?

6. How do you think farming affects biodiversity?

What's Going On?

In a natural community, very few species are abundant. As a result, most successful communities show a relatively high biodiversity index. Communities in grasslands, forests, shrubs, or deserts show a variety of species. In this experiment, you examined a nearby outdoor community. If the community you examined is highly impacted by humans, such as a section of grassy lawn on a school campus, it displayed relatively low biodiversity. In the case of a lawn, one plant species dominates. The diversity of organisms that live in and on the soil may also be low because of fertilizers, pesticides, and foot traffic.

Biodiversity in communities is determined by three factors: space, time, and feeding. If the community space has numerous layers, whether they are vertical or horizontal, diversity increases. For example, a forest has several layers beginning on the floor and moving to the top of the canopy. Layers provide plenty of *microhabitats* for organisms to exploit. Animals in a layered community can section off small areas where they can live, making it possible for many species to coexist. Changes in use based on time also increases diversity. Two species of plants can live in the same area if one blooms and grows in the spring, while the other does so in the fall. In a similar way, animals that feed at night can use the same space as those that sleep at night but search for food during the day. Differences in feeding strategies also increase diversity. Some birds feed on seeds, some on insects, and other on nectar. Because they do not compete for food, all three types of birds can live in the same area.

Connections

From a global perspective, species diversity falls into gradients. The area of greatest diversity is around the tropics. Moving toward the poles, diversity decreases (see Figure 3). For example, there are many more species of insects living near the equator than there are in Canada. This diversity gradient can be explained by the fact that the Tropics are warm, humid regions with plenty of sunlight. Such areas support more types of plants than cool, dry ones. A region with a high diversity of plants can feed many types of *herbivores*. Likewise, the greater the number of herbivores, the more *carnivores* an area will support.

In oceans, diversity decreases with distance from the continents. Near the continents, food is abundant and there are many types of habitats. Runoff from land carries minerals and nutrients into the waters. Shallow, coastal areas provide beds of seagrasses and kelp that provide places to hide, nesting areas, and an abundance of food. Far out to sea where water is deep, light cannot penetrate to the bottom to support plant life. The deep seafloor is generally uniform, providing animals with few places to live.

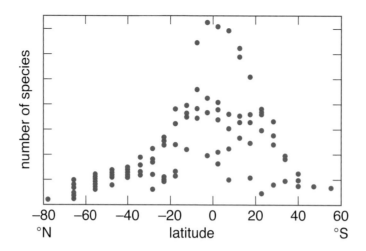

Figure 3

Species diversity is richest near the equator.

Want to Know More?

See appendix for Our Findings.

Further Reading

Bryant, Peter J. "Biodiversity and Conservation," University of California, Irvine, 2005. Available online. URL: http://darwin.bio.uci.edu/~sustain/bio65/Titlpage.htm. Accessed July 26, 2009. Bryant's hypertext book tells about the value of biodiversity and methods of preserving it.

Duffy, J. Emmett. "Biodiversity," October 30, 2007. *Encyclopedia of Earth*. Available online. URL: http://www.eoearth.org/article/Biodiversity. Accessed July 21, 2009. Duffy defines biodiversity and explains some of the problems scientists face in locating and identifying new species.

Sponsel, Leslie E. "Sacred Places and Biodiversity Conservation." Earth Portal. Available online. URL: http://www.earthportal.org/?p=399. Accessed July 26, 2009. Sponsel explains how some places of cultural significance have been protected and maintain their ancient biodiversity.

3. Monitoring Vegetative Cover

Topic

Scientists measure the amount of plant cover to understand the ecological factors of an area.

Introduction

A stroll outdoors may take you over bare soil or over plant material covering the soil. For ecologists, this is an important distinction. Ecologists study *cover*, the area of a surface that supports plant life. Cover is usually described as a percent of the area. By analyzing cover, ecologists learn two things about a region: the types of plants that are dominant and the amount of moisture that is available to plants and animals. Soil that is covered in living or dead plant matter can hold more water than bare soil. In addition, cover reduces erosion, preventing the loss of soil and the nutrients it holds.

Plants create four basic types of cover: basal, *canopy*, foliar, and ground. Basal cover refers to the proportion of ground covered by the base or trunk of the plant. Canopy is the area that is influenced by any part of the plant, including the outmost edge of the leaves. Foliar cover is related to the vertical part of the plant, and ground cover is the material that spreads across the surface of the soil.

In this experiment, you will compare two methods for analyzing ground cover. Based on the methods, you and your laboratory group will write a procedure for finding percentage of ground cover. You will swap procedures with those of another lab group, then carry out the other group's procedure in an outdoor area.

Time Required

55 minutes for part A
55 minutes for part B

Materials

- ➡ large index card
- ➡ scissors
- ➡ 2 metersticks
- ➡ string
- ➡ tape
- ➡ small metric ruler
- ➡ science notebook

Safety Note Please review and follow the safety guidelines at the beginning of this volume.

Procedure, Part A

1. Answer Analysis question 1.

2. Working with a partner, examine Figure 1, which represents a small plot that measures 1 square yard (yd) (0.8 square meters [m]). The plot contains some plants and rocks.

3. Use the estimating method of finding the percentage of plants covering the soil in this plot. To do so:

   a. Copy Data Table 1 in your science notebook.

   b. Cut a large index card in half.

   c. Cut out the middle of each half card so that you have two frames like the ones shown in Figure 2. Label one frame "A" and the other "B."

   d. Randomly toss the two frames on Figure 1. (Do not let the frames overlap.)

   e. Examine the area of the plot outlined by frame A. Estimate the percentage of the area within the frame that is covered by plants. To help you estimate, imagine moving all of the plants to one side within the frame. Would the plants cover 25 percent of the area? Would they cover 50 percent of the area? Once you have made your estimate, record it on Data Table 1 on the row labeled Frame A and the column titled Round 1.

   f. Repeat step e with frame B. Record your estimate on the row labeled Frame B and the column titled Round 1.

Figure 1

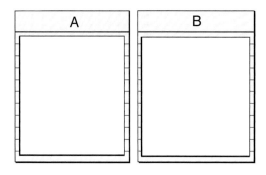

Figure 2

4. Repeat step 2, d through e, two more times. Record your estimates in the rows for Round 2 and Round 3.

5. Find the average of all three rounds for both frames. Record averages in the last column.

6. Find the average of frame A and frame B. This represents your estimated percentage of plant cover.

7. Answer Analysis question 2.

Data Table 1				
	Round 1	**Round 2**	**Round 3**	**Average**
Frame A				
Frame B				

8. Use the point method to find the percentage of plant cover in the same plot. To do so:

   a. Copy Data Table 2 in your science notebook. Leave space to add more columns to the data table if you need them.

   b. Lay a metric ruler lengthwise across the plot. You can position the ruler any way you like.

   c. Every 2 centimeters (cm), touch the point of your pencil to the plot. Notice whether you have touched a plant or not. Touching a plant is described as a "hit." Touching anything else is described as a "miss." As you work your way across the plot, put a check in the "hit" row if you touch a plant. Put a check in the "miss" row if you do not touch a plant.

Data Table 2

	2 cm	4 cm	6 cm	8 cm	10 cm	12 cm	14 cm	16 cm	18 cm	20cm	22 cm
Hit											
Miss											

   d. Find the percentage of plant cover by using the formula:

$$\text{percentage} = \frac{\text{number of hits}}{\text{total of hits and misses}} \times 100$$

9. Based on the methods you have learned about in this experiment, write a procedure for finding the percentage of plant cover in a square meter plot near your school. Your procedure should include:

   a. a materials list

   b. step-by-step directions on what to do

   Be sure your procedure is neat and easy to read because another lab group will use it to find the percentage of plants in a plot near your school.

10. When you finish writing your procedure, show it to your teacher. If you receive approval, you are finished with part A of the experiment. If you do not receive approval, make the recommended changes and resubmit the procedure to your teacher.

11. Answer Analysis question 3.

Procedure, Part B

1. Follow your teacher to an outdoor area.
2. Swap your procedure for finding ground cover with one written by another lab group.
3. Follow the procedure, recording data in your science notebook.
4. Answer Analysis questions 4 and 5.

Analysis

1. Why do ecologists study the cover on soil?
2. In part A, which technique do you think was more accurate, the estimating method or point method? Explain your reasoning.
3. What problems did you encounter when writing your procedure? How did you and your lab partner overcome these problems?
4. What problems did you encounter when carrying out the procedure written by another lab group? How did you and your partner overcome these problems?
5. Examine Figure 3, which shows a long piece a string called a transect line along which several random points were examined.

    a. How many points were examined along the transect line?

    b. How many points were "hits?"

    c. What percentage of the points were hits? To find out, use the formula

    $$\text{percentage hits} = \frac{\text{hits}}{\text{total points examined}} \times 100$$

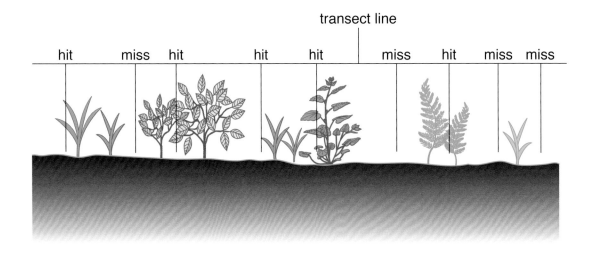

Figure 3

What's Going On?

Ecologists and land managers who manage ecosystems routinely monitor cover. Monitoring can alert ecologists to problems in the early stages. For example, an *invasive plant* that moves into a forest ecosystem is much easier to deal with when its population in relatively small. In some cases, volunteers can band together and simply pull up the unwanted invaders. As a result, *native species* will not be threatened.

Estimates and point techniques are just two of the ways land managers watch for unwanted plants and count populations of desirable or rare organisms. Another system, the step-point method, is especially useful in grasslands and shrublands. In this technique, the manager uses a compass to set a straight line across an area of study, then follows the line. The manager attaches a "pin" to his boot, a small piece of metal or plastic that projects on the outside. As he walks, the manager counts his steps and stops at regular intervals. At each stop, he records the plant that the pin is touching as a "hit." If the pin is not touching anything, the stop is recorded as a "miss." A more challenging job is to measure the vegetation in a layered environment. In a forest, for example, the canopy may be several meters above the observer's head. In this case, at each stop along the way the manager must examine the plants at the pin and everything above the pin.

Connections

Plant monitoring programs can help ecologists locate and remove unwanted organisms. In the western United States, ecologists keep watch on the growth and spread of yellow star thistle (*Centaurea solstitialis*). Native to the Mediterranean region, the plant was accidently imported into California in the early 1800s. Today, the yellow star thistle has invaded millions of acres of pasture in California, Oregon, and Washington. The short, prickly plant thrives in barren, open areas where there is little cover, so it will quickly take over poorly tended pastures. Cattle can eat it, but the plant serves as a poor source of nutrients. In horses, the weed causes a fatal condition known as "chewing disease" that damages the nervous system.

Management strategies for any type of unwanted plant include prevention, containment, and control. Prevention keeps the seeds from spreading into unaffected areas. One of the simplest prevention methods for yellow star thistle is to avoid overgrazing of pasture lands. When native plants are not eaten to their roots, star thistles cannot establish a population. Once an unwanted population develops, land managers work to contain it. Pesticides are applied to kill the weeds. Afterward, the area is routinely monitored to watch for survivors. In addition, regions that are adjacent to the affected area must also be monitored on a regular basis. For long-term success, a program of control is put into place. Land managers must continue to examine regions for the weed, spray it with pesticides when it is found, and plant desirable native grasses to keep it from finding a good habitat.

Want to Know More?

See appendix for Our Findings.

Further Reading

Elzinga, Caryl L., Daniel W. Salzer, and John W. Willoughby. "Measuring and Monitoring Plant Populations." Bureau of Land Management. Available online. URL: http://www.blm.gov/nstc/library/pdf/MeasAndMon.pdf. Accessed July 26, 2009. In this extensive manual on plant monitoring, the authors provide details of methods of assessing cover.

Limestone Pavement Conservation. "Plant Ecology." Available online. URL: http://www.limestone-pavements.org.uk/ecology.html. Accessed August 9, 2009. Limestone pavement is a threatened habitat in the United Kingdom that is under protection. The plant cover in this habitat has been extensively studied and the ecology is described on this Web site.

Seefeldt, Steven S., and D. Terrance Booth. "Measuring Plant Cover in Sagebrush Steppe Rangelands: A Comparison of Methods." Originally published in *Environmental Management*, Volume 37, Number 5, pages 703-711. Available online. URL: http://www.ars.usda.gov/SP2UserFiles/Place/54090000/BoothPDF/29.%20Measuring%20Plantcover%20in%20Sagebrush%20steppe.pdf. In this study, scientists compare new techniques for estimating ground cover in Wyoming.

4. Leaf Area Affects Primary Productivity

Topic

Leaf area provides information on the productivity of plants in an ecosystem.

Introduction

In nearly all ecosystems, plants are the primary producers, the *autotrophs* that form the base of *food chains*. The leaves of plants contain *chlorophyll,* a pigment that can capture the Sun's energy. Within chlorophyll, glucose is manufactured from carbon dioxide and water vapor in the process of *photosynthesis*. The equation for photosynthesis is:

$$6\ CO_2 + 6\ H_2O \rightarrow C_6H_{12}O_6 + 6\ O_2$$

Plants obtain the carbon dioxide and water vapor for photosynthesis through small openings in the leaves called *stomata*. The minerals and additional water they need are taken up through their roots (see Figure 1). Glucose is used either to perform work or to make the complex molecules that are found in all living things, carbohydrates, proteins, lipids, and nucleic acids.

The rate at which the producers create useful energy is known as primary production. *Gross primary production* (GPP) refers to the amount of carbon dioxide that is "fixed," or converted from carbon dioxide gas to glucose by photosynthesis. Some of this glucose is used to carry out *cellular respiration*, the process in which glucose is changed to energy to carry out life processes. The equation for cellular respiration is:

$$6\ O_2 + C_6H_{12}O_6 \rightarrow 6\ CO_2 + 6\ H_2O$$

Net primary production (NPP) is the amount of primary production after the cost of cellular respiration in plants is deducted. Measuring NPP tells you how much organic material has been synthesized from inorganic compounds and made available to the ecosystem. Measured in units of mass/area/time, NPP in terrestrial ecosystems is usually expressed in grams of carbon per square meter per year.

Ecologists are interested in NPP because it helps them understand the balance of carbon dioxide in ecosystems. One way to estimate primary production is by finding the leaf area of the ecosystem. In this experiment, you will compare the leaf area, and therefore the productivity, of two different kinds of plants in the same ecosystem.

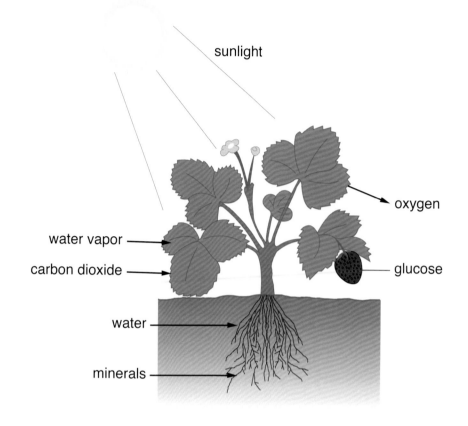

Figure 1

Time Required

65 minutes

Materials

- ruler
- calculator
- science notebook

Safety Note   Please review and follow the safety guidelines at the beginning of this volume.

Procedure

1. Follow your teacher to an outdoor area.

2. Select two different deciduous plants of about the same size. Ideally, chose two plants that are at least 2 feet (ft) (0.6 meters [m]) tall but not so tall that you cannot see the tops. For example, you might select a small oak tree and a small beech tree. Or you could select two different shrubs that are planted at the school's foundation. If you do not know the names of the plants, call one "A" and the other "B."

3. Count the number of leaves on an average-size limb of plant A. Record the number of leaves in your science notebook.

4. Count the number of limbs on plant A. Record the number of limbs in your science notebook.

5. Pick an average-size leaf from plant A. To determine the leaf's approximate surface area, measure its greatest length by its greatest width and multiply the measurements (see Figure 2). Record the area of the leaf in your science notebook.

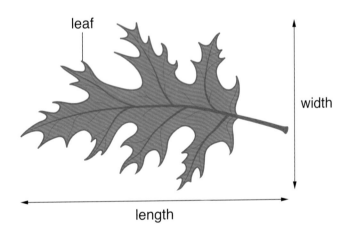

Figure 2

6. Find the total area of the leaves on plant A. To do so:

   a. Multiply the area of one leaf by the number of leaves on a limb.

   b. Multiply the number of leaves on a limb by the number of limbs on the plant.

   Record the total leaf area of plant A in your science notebook.

7. Repeat steps 2 through 6 for plant B.

Analysis

1. What is the difference in GPP and NPP?
2. Photosynthesis and cellular respiration are two biochemical processes carried out by plants. Which process uses energy? Which process stores energy?
3. Scientists use several methods of finding the total leaf area of a plant. In the direct method all of the leaves of the plant are removed and measured, and the area of each is recorded. What is one advantage of this method? What is one disadvantage?
4. How do you think a drought might change the productivity of a plant?
5. Which of the plants you measured had: (a) the largest leaves? (b) the most leaves? (c) the largest leaf area?
6. Suggest a way to find the area of one leaf accurately.

What's Going On?

Energy flows through ecosystems, beginning with primary producers and moving to *herbivores,* then *carnivores.* In terrestrial ecosystems, the leaves of plants are the primary photosynthetic organs. In aquatic environments, algae fill this role. Some algae are unicellular, while others are large, multicellular organisms. All of the photosynthetic organisms on Earth capture and use only about 0.06 percent of the solar energy that falls on them. The organisms use some of this captured energy to support their own life processes. The amount of energy that is made available to primary consumers is about 0.06 percent of the available solar energy.

Scientists have calculated that green organisms are not very efficient energy converters. Only about 2 percent of the Sun's energy that strikes a plant or alga is changed to glucose. The glucose made by plants determines how much energy is available in ecosystems and therefore limits how many animals can live there.

Connections

NPP is not the same in all ecosystems. Factors that affect productivity include the availability of carbon dioxide, sunlight, and nutrients. Figure 3 shows the NPP of each type of ecosystem on Earth. Three types of ecosystems stand out as very high producers: estuaries, saltwater marshes, and tropical rain forests.

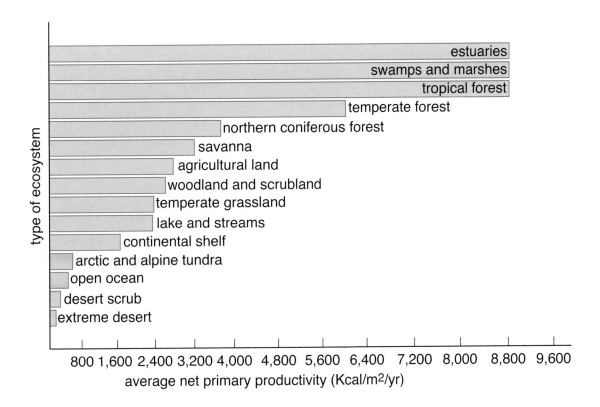

Figure 3

Average net primary production in different ecologies

Figure 3 shows that the patterns of productivity vary by climate. The most-productive systems are in relatively warm regions that have plenty of moisture and high levels of nitrogen, an essential nutrient. Less-productive ecosystems, like the tundra and desert, lack heat energy and water. Agricultural ecosystems are also very productive because their water needs can be met with irrigation and their nutrients requirements with fertilizers.

Since the arrival of humans on Earth, natural ecosystems have undergone changes. Humans change forests to pastures and farms to meet their needs. Humans now control about 40 percent of the terrestrial NPP, a phenomenon known as *human appropriation of net primary productivity,* or HANPP. Never in Earth's history has one species so dominated the use of space and organisms. The price of this domination is linked to pollution, loss of other species, and *global warming*.

Want to Know More?
See appendix for Our Findings.

Further Reading

Haberl, Helmut, Karl-Heinz Erb, and Fridolin Krausmann. "Global human appropriation of net primary production (HANPP)," December 10, 2008. Available online. URL: http://www.eoearth.org/article/Global_human_appropriation_of_net_primary_production_(HANPP). Accessed July 27, 2009. The authors explain how humans have changed ecosystems to raise animals and crops for their use.

NASA. "Earth Observatory." Available online. URL: http://earthobservatory.nasa.gov/GlobalMaps/view.php?d1=MOD17A2_M_PSN#. Accessed July 27, 2009. NASA provides an interactive globe that shows how primary productivity has changed since 2000.

University of Michigan. "The Flow of Energy: Primary Production to Higher Trophic Levels," October 31, 2008. Available online. URL: http://www.globalchange.umich.edu/globalchange1/current/lectures/kling/energyflow/energyflow.html. Accessed July 26, 2009. The authors explain the roles of primary production in a variety of ecosystems.

5. Diversity in Soil Ecosystems

Topic

Soil ecosystems vary depending on availability of water and nutrients and the condition of the soil.

Introduction

All organisms have the same basic requirements for life: food, water, and space for living. Most large organisms also require oxygen. The soil provides an environment for millions of different types of living things. The organisms that live in the soil have the same needs as those on the surface.

As surface dwellers, humans may not realize that life in the soil has many benefits. Soil organisms enjoy a climate that is relatively quiet and stable compared to the surface. Soil inhabitants are protected from extremes in temperature, solar radiation, drying, and wind. On the other hand, life underground is not perfect and soil dwellers face some problems. For example, the soil offers little space and it makes movement difficult.

Soils vary tremendously in mineral composition and pore space so they provide a wide variety of habitats. Bacteria, both *aerobic* and *anaerobic* types, are abundant in soil. Protists, organisms that are primarily unicellular, are also numerous. Some of the most easily visible soil inhabitants are the *invertebrates*, an extremely large group of animals that lacks backbones. Earthworms, one of soil's best known residents, are invertebrates that channel through soil, consume dead organic matter, and excrete indigestible particles. Mites, snails, slugs, insect larvae, and beetles are just a few other animals (see Figure 1). In addition, plants send their roots deep into soil, providing anchors as well as access to water and minerals. Fungi spread tiny, threadlike filaments throughout soil, especially in regions where dead organic matter is plentiful.

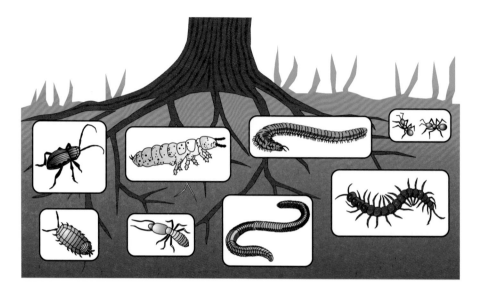

Figure 1

The soil is inhabited by a wide variety of organisms.

The amount of space between soil particles, the pore space, determines how much room is available for organisms. Pore space also affects the availability of oxygen and water. Most soil organisms spend their time in the pore spaces. For this reason, the size of pore spaces determines which organisms can live in a plot of soil. In this experiment, you will examine soil in three sites and then develop an experiment to collect and examine the soil organisms at each site.

Time Required

45 minutes for part A
65 minutes for part B

Materials

- shovel
- ruler
- paper cup
- electronic scale or triple-beam balance
- 100 milliliter (ml) graduated cylinder
- weighing boat

- Berlese funnel
- invertebrate pitfall trap
- dishpan
- forceps
- collecting bottle
- about 200 ml of ethanol
- dissecting microscope or magnifying glass
- small soil corer
- access to water
- science notebook

Safety Note Please review and follow the safety guidelines at the beginning of this volume.

Procedure, Part A

1. Follow your teacher on a tour of several outdoor areas that have a variety of soil types. At each site:

   a. Assess the amount of moisture in the soil. To do so, dig about 2 inches (in.) (5 centimeters [cm]) below the surface and pick up a handful of soil. Squeeze the soil in your hand to form a ball. Open your hand to see if the ball remains intact. If it does, describe the soil as *damp*. If it falls apart after a few minutes, describe the soil as *moderate*. If the ball of soil falls apart immediately, describe the soil as *dry*. Record the amount of moisture on Data Table 1.

   b. Determine the temperature of the soil by carefully inserting a soil thermometer to a depth of about 2 in. (5 cm). After a minute, read the temperature and record the temperature on Data Table 1.

   c. Notice the color of the soil. Describe the color on Data Table 1.

   d. Determine the density of a soil core sample. Generally, compacted soil is denser than loose soil. Use the corer to collect a sample of soil. Place the soil sample in a paper cup. When you return to the classroom, use the graduated cylinder to measure 100 ml of soil. Pour the soil into a *weighing boat*. Tare the scale and find the weight of the soil. Calculate the density using the formula:

$$D = \frac{m}{v}$$

where *D* is density, *m* is mass, and *v* is volume.

Record the density on Data Table 1.

Data Table 1					
	Moisture	**Temperature**	**Color**	**Density**	**Other notes**
Site 1					
Site 2					
Site 3					

2. Answer Analysis questions 1 and 2.

Procedure, Part B

1. Based on the information you gathered from the soil sites, develop a hypothesis about which of the three soil sites has the most diverse community of invertebrates. Write your hypothesis in your science notebook.

2. Your job is to design and perform an experiment to test your hypothesis. You can use any of the supplies provided by your teacher, but you may not need to use all of them.

3. Before you conduct your experiment, decide exactly what you are going to do. Write the steps you plan to take (your experimental procedure) and the materials you plan to use (materials list) on Data Table 2. Show your procedure and materials list to the teacher. If you get teacher approval, proceed with your experiment. If not, modify your work and show it to your teacher again.

4. Once you have teacher approval, assemble the materials you need and begin your procedure.

Data Table 2	
Your experimental procedure	
Your materials list	
Teacher's approval	

5. Collect your results on a data table of your own design.

6. Answer Analysis questions 3 through 6.

Analysis

1. What do soil invertebrates need to live?

2. Based on your observations in part A, which soil site, A, B, or C, do you think will have the most diverse population of invertebrates? Explain your reasoning.

3. How did you collect invertebrates at each soil site?

4. Did your hypothesis prove to be true or false?

5. Describe three of the most common organisms you found in your soil samples.

6. Based on this experiment, which site has the greatest *biodiversity*, or variety of living things?

What's Going On?

In this experiment, you examined the soil and the organisms in three different sites. The degree of soil compaction varied at each site. Soil compaction occurs when soil particles are pressed close together, reducing the pore space (see Figure 2). Soil compaction can develop in a region where a foot path receives a lot of traffic, in an area where livestock live, or in a trail where bikes, motorcycles, cars, and other vehicles routinely travel.

By collecting and examining soil inhabitants, you found that highly compacted or dense soil supports fewer organisms than loose soil. Compacted soil supports fewer numbers and types of organisms for several reasons. When soil particles are close together, very little oxygen-carrying air can circulate. In addition, water does not percolate into the soil easily. However, once soil spaces become saturated, it takes a long time for the water to drain off. Plant roots must exert much more force to push through compacted soil than through loose soil. As a result, some plants cannot survive.

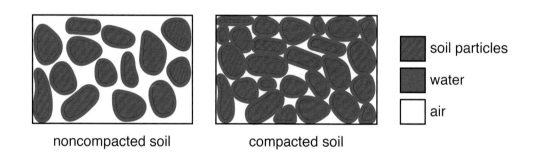

noncompacted soil   compacted soil

Figure 2

Connections

Soils develop from the *weathering* of rocks and mineral. Because they are exposed to water, wind, and varying temperatures, rocks break apart. Water combines with carbon dioxide to form *carbonic acid*, a reactive compound that chemically speeds rock weathering. Eventually, weathering produces small particles that either stay in place or are carried to new locations.

Once rock is broken into loose material, plants appear and speed soil production in several ways. The roots of plants create spaces and help fragment rocks and minerals. Plants roots capture minerals that are deep in the soil and bring them close to the surface. Through photosynthesis, plants convert carbon dioxide and water vapor to carbon compounds. Some of these compounds become incorporated in the soil. Eventually, carbon compounds are decomposed by fungal and microbial soil residents. Other plant matter serves as food for small animals. As they feed, these organisms produce metabolic waste material that enters the soil. In addition, their bodies eventually become incorporated in soil. The portion of soil that is made up of organic matter is known as *humus*. Soil is an important link between minerals and organic matter that acts as a foundation for most food webs.

Want to Know More?

See appendix for Our Findings.

Further Reading

Ecoplexity. "Modeling the Basic Soil Ecosystem," Portland State University, 2009. Available online. URL: http://ecoplexity.org/soil_model. Accessed July 28, 2009. This tutorial describes some soil organisms and explains their roles in soil ecosystems.

Ramel, Gordon. "The Soil Makers," May 4, 2009. Available online. URL: http://www.earthlife.net/insects/soileco.html. Accessed July 28, 2009. Ramel's Web site on soil ecology includes a list of organisms one might find living in the soil.

University of Minnesota. "Soil Biology and Soil Management," 2002. Available online. URL: http://www.extension.umn.edu/distribution/ cropsystems/components/7403_02.html. Accessed July 27, 2009. Soil communities support bacteria, protists, fungi, plant parts, and a variety of animals such as earthworms, nematodes, insect larvae, and insects.

6. Food Webs

Topic

The energy captured by plants is passed on to other organisms in ecosystems.

Introduction

The Earth receives plenty of radiant energy from the Sun. However, many organisms, including animals and fungi, cannot use solar energy. Plants and other organisms that contain chlorophyll are the only ones that can "fix" solar energy through *photosynthesis*. By fixing energy, plants convert solar radiation into the chemical energy of glucose and other compounds. The energy captured and stored in plants is passed on to other organisms in a series of feeding relationships known as a *food chain*. A food chain shows a sequence of species that are connected by arrows. The direction of the arrows indicates which species serve as food for another. In the food chain shown in Figure 1, grass serves as food for an insect, which is fed on by a bird.

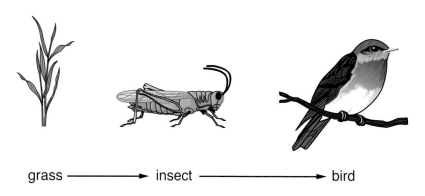

grass ⟶ insect ⟶ bird

Figure 1

You know that insects eat more than grass and that birds feed on a variety of organisms. In an ecosystem, consumers share resources, especially the *producers*. Grass provides food for a variety of organisms, some of which eat the blades, while others dine on stems, roots, or seeds. A *food web* shows all of the feeding relationships in an ecosystem.

Food webs have several basic components: producers, primary consumers, secondary consumers, tertiary consumers, and decomposers. The organisms that eat producers are known as primary consumers or *herbivores*. This group of organisms includes deer, rabbits, and squirrels. Herbivores have special adaptations for digesting cellulose, a very tough fiber in plants. Some herbivores have specialized grinding teeth, while others have complex stomachs, very long intestines, or bacteria in their digestive systems that secrete cellulose-digesting enzymes. Herbivores are fed on by secondary consumers or *carnivores*, animals that eat other animals. Carnivores are adapted for their roles as flesh eaters. Hawks and eagles have sharp talons for killing and grasping. Mammalian carnivores have sharp teeth for tearing meat and very few teeth for grinding.

Not all consumers fall into these two groups. Some consumers can eat plant parts as well as animals. *Omnivores* are organisms that dine on both *trophic*, or feeding, levels. Some omnivores also act as *scavengers*, animals that eat dead plants and animals. Coyotes will eat small animals, but they also scavenge and eat fruits and berries. For many omnivores, feeding habits vary with season and food availability.

The final feeding level in a food chain is made up of *decomposers*. These organisms break down dead tissue and body wastes and convert them into nutrients that are accessible to other organisms. Bacteria and fungi are two types of decomposers found in most food chains. In this experiment, you will analyze several prairie food chains and use them to construct a food web.

Time Required

55 minutes

Materials

➥ scissors

➥ science notebook

Safety Note   Please review and follow the safety guidelines at the beginning of this volume.

Procedure

1. Use scissors to cut out the organisms and arrows in Figure 2. Set aside the blank boxes for now.

2. Use the Internet or reference books to research what the animals in Figure 2 eat.

3. On your desktop, arrange the organisms into five different food chains. Connect each trophic level within a food chain with an arrow. The arrow should indicate the direction in which energy moves through the food chain. Food chains can contain three or four organisms. (You should not have any organisms left over.) If necessary, draw some additional arrows.

4. Answer Analysis questions 1 and 2.

5. Rearrange the five food chains into one large food web.

6. In the blank boxes, draw and name two decomposers.

7. Add the decomposers to your food web. If necessary, draw some additional arrows to accommodate the decomposers.

8. Answer Analysis questions 3 through 9.

Analysis

1. What kind of organism formed the base of each food chain?

2. In what direction does energy move through a food chain: consumer to producer or producer to consumer?

3. Based on what you know about food chains, draw an aquatic food chain that includes the organisms in the following data table:

Data Table	
zooplankton (small animals floating in the water)	seals
whales	large fish
small fish	phytoplankton (small, plant-like organisms floating in the water)

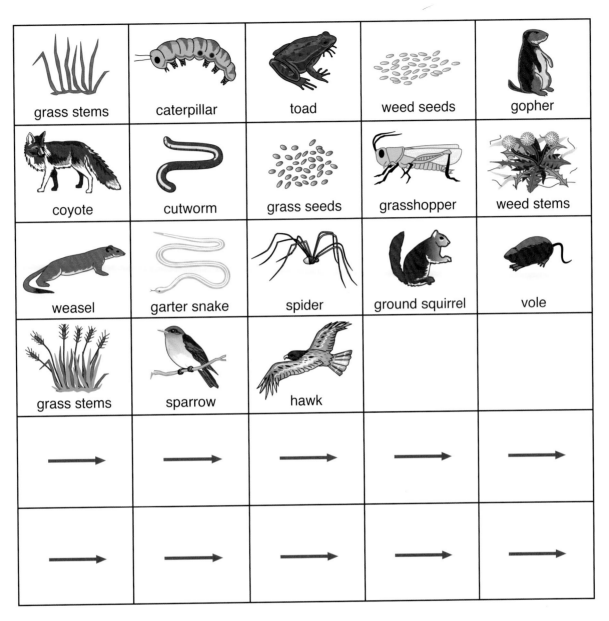

Figure 2

4. How many trophic levels are in the food chain you drew for question 3?

5. What two decomposers did you add to the food web in procedure step 5?

6. Why are decomposers needed in food webs?

7. What is the role of producers in a food chain or food web?

8. The food web you created in this experiment does not contain any scavengers. What is the role of scavengers in an ecosystem?

9. List the organisms in your food web by category:
   a. producers
   b. primary consumers
   c. secondary consumers
   d. tertiary consumers

What's Going On?

The two major types of food chains are the grazing food chain and the detrital food chain. *Detritus* is dead organic matter. Some of the primary consumers in grazing food chains include deer or elk feeding in a meadow, rabbits eating grasses, and grasshoppers devouring leaves. Even though these are the most obvious food chains, they are not the most common. Detrital food chains form the majority of paths through which energy is channeled. In the prairie, about three-fourths of the plant matter is returned to the soil where it decays. In addition, a large percentage of the plant matter consumed by herbivores is returned to the soil as feces.

In a detrital food chain, organisms that eat dead plant and animal matter are referred to as detritivores or *saprophages*. The primary saprophages are microscopic bacteria and fungi. Millipedes, mites, earthworms, slugs, and crickets are a few of the invertebrates that serve as saprophages. These animals are fed on by carnivorous invertebrates like spiders and beetles. The macrosaprophages and microsaprophages support each other. The former shred and break apart large pieces of material, making it available to microbes and fungi. The microsaprophages digest the organic matter and concentrate it into larger particles that macrosaprophages eat. After consuming this food, the larger organisms produce fecal pellets that are feed on by the microscopic community.

Connections

A food chain shows the feeding relationships among organisms. Each step of the chain represents a trophic level. For example, animals that feed on plants represent one trophic level. Animals that eat other animals represent another trophic level. Many animals feed on multiple trophic levels because food supplies vary.

As one organism consumes another, it gains the energy needed to support life. Plants, the base of most food chains, are able to convert about one percent of the Sun's energy that falls on them into stored energy or food. When a herbivore such as a mouse feeds on a plant, the mouse only assimilates about 10 percent of the energy originally stored by the plant. The plant used up much of the energy to carry out respiration. In addition, energy was lost to the plant's environment as heat. When a weasel eats the mouse, the predator only gains about 10 percent of the mouse's energy. So, if the mouse consumes 1,000 kilocalories of energy from the plant, the weasel could only gain 100 kilocalories. Eventually, the amount of available energy in a food chain is so small that no more organisms can be supported.

Want to Know More?

See appendix for Our Findings.

Further Reading

Chesapeake Bay Program. "Food Web," July 29, 2009. Available online. URL: http://www.chesapeakebay.net/foodweb.aspx?menuitem=15903. Accessed August 30, 2009. The Chesapeake Bay Program, a regional partnership to restore the bay, helps educate the public on the ecology of the bay system. This Web page gives examples of food webs in the bay.

Duffy, J. Emmett. "Food Web," *Encyclopedia of Earth,* January 7, 2008. Available online. URL:http://www.eoearth.org/article/Food_web. Accessed October 7, 2009. Duffy discusses the transfer of energy and the pyramid of numbers in food chains.

Ward, Paul. "Whales and Food Webs," Cool Antarctica, 2001. Available online. URL: http://www.coolantarctica.com/Antarctica%20fact%20file/wildlife/whales/food%20web.htm. Accessed August 30, 2009. On this Web site, Paul Ward explains the food webs and food chains of Antarctica.

7. Biome Learning Centers

Topic

Biomes are regions that have characteristic climates, plants, and animals.

Introduction

You live in a *biome*, a region that has distinctive characteristics due to its climate and geography. Two of the most fundamental determinants of a biome's climate are temperature and the amount of precipitation. The resulting climate determines the types of plants and animals that survive there. The major terrestrial biomes are deserts, tundras, taigas, temperate deciduous forests, grasslands, savannas, temperate rain forests, temperate seasonal forests, and tropical rain forests. Figure 1 shows the mean annual temperature in Celsius and the mean annual precipitation in centimeters for the terrestrial biomes.

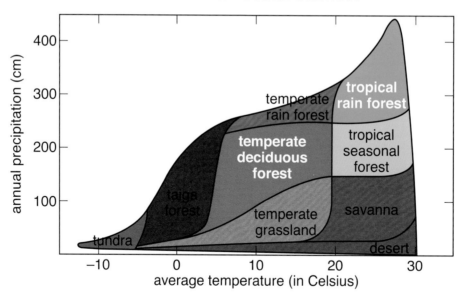

Figure 1

Mean annual temperature and precipitaion of biomes

Within each biome are unique communities of organisms that share the space and the resources. Because the organisms and the environment are interconnected, changes to any part of the biome can affect all other parts. In this experiment, you will become an expert on the *abiotic*, or nonliving, and *biotic*, or living, parts of one biome. You will use your expertise to construct a learning center that the entire class can enjoy.

Time Required

55 minutes for part A
two 55-minute periods for part B
45 minutes for part C

Materials

- ⟜ access to the Internet or books on biomes
- ⟜ printer (optional)
- ⟜ art supplies (such as cardboard, construction paper, paint, glue, markers, tape, paper-mache, yarn, and clay)
- ⟜ ruler
- ⟜ scissors
- ⟜ cardboard box
- ⟜ trifold display board
- ⟜ science notebook

Safety Note   Please review and follow the safety guidelines at the beginning of this volume.

Procedure, Part A

1. Working in groups of two or three, use the Internet or books on biomes to research the biome assigned to you by your teacher. Learn all you can about the biome and record your findings in your science notebook. In particular, you should write down details about the following:

   a. climate and weather of the region

   b. plants and animals of the region

   c. how plants and animals are adapted to the biomes

    d. geographical locations of the biome

    e. kind of terrain found in your region

    f. elevation of the biome

    Record your findings in your science notebook.

  2. List some of the geographical locations of your biome and color them on the world map in Figure 2.

  3. Sketch, trace, or print two or more pictures that represent the plants, animals, and landscape of the biome.

Procedure, Part B

  1. Working with your group, create a biome display that will act as a learning center for your classmates. Your learning center should be interesting and attractive and provide accurate, educational material. All of the required information must be displayed in a way that makes it easy for other students to study it. Students will use your display to answer the Analysis questions.

  2. The data table contains a rubric shows the requirements for the learning centers and the points you can earn by meeting each requirement. Examine this rubric closely before you begin making your learning center. Notice that your learning station must include the following:

    a. a written description of biotic and abiotic factors in the biome

    b. charts showing the temperatures (in Celsius) and precipitation (in centimeters) over 1 year

    c. lists of common plants and animals, along with pictures

    d. explanations of adaptations that help plants and animals survive in the biome

    e. a food web showing feeding relationship in the biome

    f. an energy pyramid showing how energy is transferred through the biome

    g. a vocabulary activity for your classmates

  3. Read the Analysis questions before you begin work on your center. Make sure that your center answers all of the Analysis questions that are relevant to your biome.

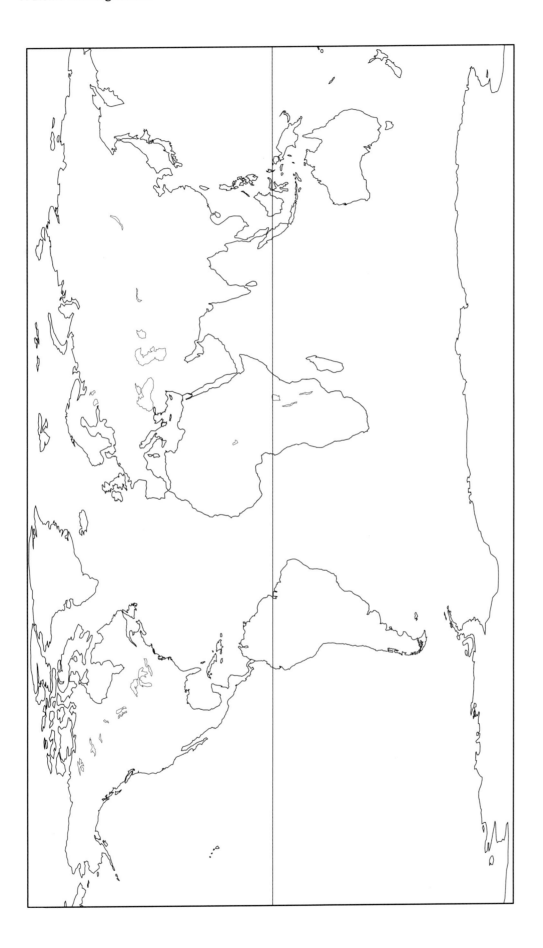

Figure 2
World map

Data Table

Names of group members_____

_____

Name of biome _____

Requirements	Points possible	Points earned
Written description (minimum 200 words) of the biome that includes the biotic and abiotic factors	20	
Chart showing the average precipitation per month for 1 year	8	
Chart showing the average temperature per month for 1 year	8	
List of the common animals in the biome (at least 10). Pictures of at least two animals.	8	
List of the common plants in the biome (at least 10). Pictures of at least two plants.	8	
Explanation of plant and animal adaptations for the biome	8	
Food web showing the feeding relationships of at least five plants and five animals	8	
Energy pyramid for the biome using names of plants and animals, with labels: producers, primary consumers, secondary consumers, tertiary consumers	8	
Vocabulary activity that contains at least 15 terms that are important to your biome. Examples of vocabulary activities are puzzles, Frayer diagrams, and matching activities	8	
Biome display is attractive	8	
Biome display is neat	8	
Total	100	

Procedure, Part C

1. Visit each biome learning station to carry out an assessment. Use a copy of the rubric to assess the station. When you have completed your assessment, give the rubric to the teacher.

2. Visit each biome learning station as a learner. Read the information provided, study the pictures, and complete the vocabulary activity.

3. Complete the Analysis questions.

Analysis

1. How long is the growing season in the tundra?
2. What is the difference between the arctic tundra and the alpine tundra?
3. In terms of rainfall, the tundra is most like what other biome?
4. How is the soil of the tundra unique?
5. What are some of the adaptations that tundra animals have to survive the cold climate?
6. What are some of the dominant plants in the tundra?
7. Describe the leaves of trees that live in the taiga.
8. How many months each year are the average temperatures below freezing in the taiga?
9. What is the largest biome?
10. Which biome has four distinct seasons?
11. Second to the rain forest, which biome gets the most rain?
12. Why do the leaves of deciduous trees fall in the autumn?
13. What causes the seasons?
14. What is the main difference between a hot and a cold desert (besides temperature)?
15. Name the four major deserts of North America.
16. What is the world's largest desert?
17. How do desert animals endure the extreme heat?
18. During the day, desert temperatures can be extremely high. However, at night, the desert can become cool. Why is this so?
19. In order to be classified as a tropical rain forest a forest must be located between what two tropics?

20. Where can you find a rain forest in the United States?

21. What are some differences in a tropical rain forest and a temperate rain forest?

22. What are the three types of grasslands found in the United States?

23. What kinds of grazing animals once dominated the U.S. prairies?

24. What is the only continent that does not have grasslands?

What's Going On?

Biomes are primarily identified by their dominant plants. Grasslands have characteristic grasses, temperature deciduous forests are wooded, and deserts support cacti and other drought-resistant plants. The diversity of life in each biome is controlled by abiotic factors such as water, nutrients, and light. In general, warm, moist biomes have more species diversity than cold, dry ones.

Adaptations to *niches* can be seen by comparing organisms that live in the same biomes in different geographical areas. For examples, all grasslands are similar in that they have plenty of grass and very little cover for predators. These regions support large grazing *ungulates*, animals with hoofs and long legs that can outrun predators. In North America, grasslands support bison and elk; in Africa one might find zebras and antelope. These different animals with similar adaptations show us how environments determine the traits of the organisms that inhabit them.

Connections

Biomes are undergoing changes due to human impacts on the world's climate. For the last decade, scientists have noticed that Arctic glaciers are melting at an accelerated rate. In addition, ice floating in the Arctic is declining and is currently at an all-time low. Researchers hypothesize that the loss of sea ice may be due to changing patterns in atmospheric pressure over the Arctic and by warming temperatures caused by the build up of *greenhouse gases*. Global warming could set off a series of changes that affect the ocean processes.

Sunlight has a different effect on liquid water and ice. Ice reflects solar energy, but liquid water absorbs it and becomes warmer. As water in the Arctic continues to warm, it melts ice at a faster than normal rate. This *positive feedback system* leads to more melting ice and more warming. If this pattern continues, some scientists fear that temperatures in deep layers of the ocean will change, which will affect climates all over the globe. Scientists have been monitoring the thickness of sea ice for the last 50 years. Ice seems to be disappearing at a rate of about 10 percent per year.

One sad consequence of glacial melting is the loss of habitat for animals that live on ice. Polar bears hunt, fish, mate, and even given birth on ice. As the ice retreats, they can no longer make a living in their normal way. As a result, many are drowning or starving to death.

Want to Know More?

See appendix for Our Findings.

Further Reading

Blue Planet. "Deciduous Forest," 2009. Available online. URL: http://www.blueplanetbiomes.org/world_biomes.htm. Accessed July 31, 2009. The Web site provides an excellent description of deciduous forests and links to pages on other biomes.

CNN.com, Planet in Peril. "Polar Bears Resort to Cannibalism as Arctic Ice Shrinks, "December 5, 2008. Available online. URL: http://www.cnn.com/2008/TECH/09/23/arctic.ice/index.html. Accessed August 2, 2009. Some scientists predict that at today's rate of loss of polar ice, the Arctic could be ice free in the summers within 5 years.

MBGnet. "What's It Like Where You Live?" 2005. Available online. URL: http://www.mbgnet.net/. Accessed July 31, 2009. Supported by the Missouri Botanical Garden, this attractive, user-friendly site discusses characteristics of the world's major biomes.

8. Surface Area Affects Body Temperature

Topic

Body size and weight affect the metabolic rate and temperature of animals.

Introduction

In an ecosystem, heat is an important *abiotic* factor. All organisms exchange heat energy with the environment. Living things absorb radiant energy from the Sun or from heat that is reflected by the Earth's surface (see Figure 1). In addition, organisms lose heat energy as a result of their metabolic activities.

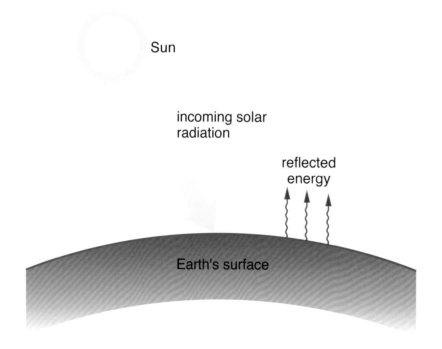

Sun

incoming solar radiation

reflected energy

Earth's surface

Figure 1

Animals can be divided into two large groups based on how their bodies deal with heat energy. *Ectotherms*, animals whose body temperature depends on the environment, are generally described as cold-blooded. Fish, amphibians, reptiles, and insects are ectotherms. *Endotherms*, or warm-blooded animals, are able to generate their own body heat. Humans fall in this category, along with other mammals and birds. The high body heat of endotherms enables them to remain active regardless of the environment's temperature. However, these animals must expend a lot of energy just to maintain their basic *metabolism*. Body size is one factor that affects metabolic rate. In this experiment, you will determine how body size affects heat loss.

Time Required

45 minutes

Materials

- 250-milliliter (ml) beaker
- 150 ml beaker
- 50 ml beaker
- 3 thermometers
- access to warm water
- clock or timer
- graph paper
- colored pencils
- science notebook

Safety Note Please review and follow the safety guidelines at the beginning of this volume.

Procedure

1. Fill the three beakers with warm water.
2. Insert a thermometer into each beaker.
3. Record the starting temperature of each beaker on Data Table 1.
4. Answer Analysis questions 1 and 2.
5. After 2 minutes (min), check and record all three temperatures again.

6. Continue checking and recording the temperatures every 2 min for 14 min.

7. Create a line graph comparing the changes in temperature over a period of 14 min. Place time in min on the X-axis and temperature in degrees on the Y-axis. Use a different color pencil for each beaker.

8. Answering Analysis questions 3 through 7.

9. To help regulate the rate at which heat is lost to the environment, some endotherms have *insulation*. For example, birds have feathers that help trap air near their bodies, keeping them warm. Many mammals have fur coats that do the same thing. Mammals that live in very cold climates also have a layer of fat to help maintain their body heat. Write an experiment to determine which is most effective in helping maintain body temperature: feathers, fur, or fat. Record your experiment on Data Table 2. Be sure that your experiment includes the following:

   a. hypothesis

   b. materials list

   c. procedure (that contains exact, step-by-step directions)

   Remember to control for all variables except for the one you want to test.

Data Table 1			
	250-ml beaker	**150-ml beaker**	**50-ml beaker**
Start			
2 minute			
4 minutes			
6 minutes			
8 minutes			
10 minutes			
12 minutes			
14 minutes			

Data Table 2

Your hypothesis	
Your materials list	
Your procedure	

Analysis

1. Which beaker do you think will cool the fastest? Explain your reasoning.

2. In this experiment, which beaker represents a:
   a. large animal
   b. medium-size animal
   c. small animal

3. Based on your experimental results, was your prediction in question 1 correct?

4. In your own words, explain the relationship between body size and heat loss.

5. Where do animals get the energy needed to carry out the basic metabolic processes?

6. Which animal do you think eats the most food per body mass each day, a small one or a large one? Why?

7. Name some of the variables that you controlled in the experiment that you wrote.

What's Going On?

In this experiment, you used a large beaker to represent a large animal and smaller beakers to represent smaller animals. You graph showed that the smaller the animal, the faster it loses heat. Your results mimic real life because as body weight increases, the metabolic rate decreases. For example, doubling body weight decreases the rate of metabolism by 75 percent. The reverse is also true, the smaller an animal's body weight, the faster its rate of metabolism. Therefore, small animals need to eat more food per unit of body weight than large ones. Shrews, small mammals that live in the leaf litter, eat an equivalent of their entire body weight each day (see Figure 2). To keep themselves fed, these animals spend almost all of their time looking for food. If a 100-pound (lb) (45.4-kilogram [kg]) teenager had the same metabolic rate, he or she would have to eat 100 lb (45.4 kg) of food each day. Scientists have calculated that the smallest an endotherm can be and still supply its energy needs is about 0.17 ounces (5 grams), the weight of a nickel.

Figure 2

A shrew is a small, warm-blooded animal.

Connections

Because ectotherms do not maintain a constant body temperature, they do not need as much food as endotherms. For this reason, ectotherms can be found in very small sizes. When a lizard or amphibian is resting, it only needs about 15 percent as much energy as a mammal of equal size. Therefore, cold-blooded animals spend more time resting, and less time feeding, than warm blooded ones.

Cold-blooded animals have some behavioral tricks for regulating the body temperatures. Amphibians, reptiles, and insects spread out in the Sun to warm their bodies. If they get too warm, the animals move to the shade. During the summer, these ectotherms can maintain a fairly constant body temperature by moving between warm and cool locations. Reptiles that live in very hot regions also raise and lower their bodies to control the amount of air circulation around them. In addition, some species dig into the soil to avoid the Sun (see Figure 3).

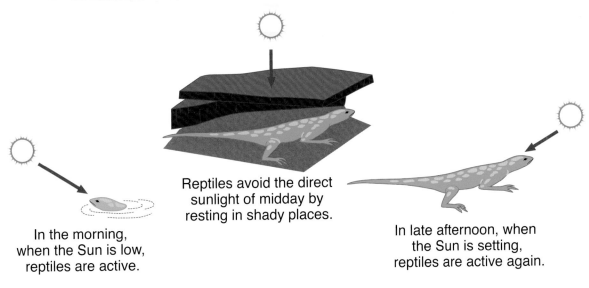

Reptiles avoid the direct sunlight of midday by resting in shady places.

In the morning, when the Sun is low, reptiles are active.

In late afternoon, when the Sun is setting, reptiles are active again.

Figure 3

Lizards have behavioral adaptations for controlling their body temperature.

Want to Know More?

See appendix for Our Findings.

Further Reading

Cornell University. Introducing biology, Individual Instruction, Unit 4, "Body Temperature Regulation," 2009. Available online. URL: http://www.biog1105-1106.org/demos/105/unit3/bodytempregulation.html. Accessed August 2, 2009. This online resource for beginning biology students explains the differences in endotherms and ectotherms.

Hermans-Killman, Linda. Cool Cosmos. "Warm and Cold-Blooded." Available online. URL: http://coolcosmos.ipac.caltech.edu/image_galleries/ir_zoo/coldwarm.html. Accessed January 2, 2010. This Web site explains the differences between warm- and cold blooded animals and shows infrared images of both.

Koehler, Kenneth. "Body Temperature Regulation," 2003. Available online. URL: http://www.rwc.uc.edu/koehler/biophys/8d.html. Accessed August 2, 2009. In this article for advanced students, Koehler, of the University of Cincinnati, relates body temperature to enzyme activity and conductivity.

University of California. "Based on Body Size, Bacteria and Elephants Have Similar Metabolism, Ecologists Find," 2005. Available online. URL: http://www.universityofcalifornia.edu/news/article/7578. Accessed August 2, 2009. This Web page reports on research study by professor Bai-Lian Li of University of California Riverside showing that when the metabolic rates of very different organisms of the same size are compared, they are similar.

9. Predator and Prey Populations

Topic

Fluctuations in the size of prey populations affect the size of predator populations.

Introduction

In ecosystems, energy is passed along food chains from producers to primary and secondary consumers. Animals that are killed and eaten by other animals are described as prey. Animals that do the killing and consuming are predators.

The sizes of prey and predators populations show characteristic fluctuations in size. More than a century ago, fur traders living in Canada who were working for the Hudson Bay Company started keeping records on the sizes of animal populations. Since that time, ecologists have followed up on their work. A graph of changes in populations of a prey and its predator, the snowshoe hare and Canadian lynx, can be seen in Figure 1.

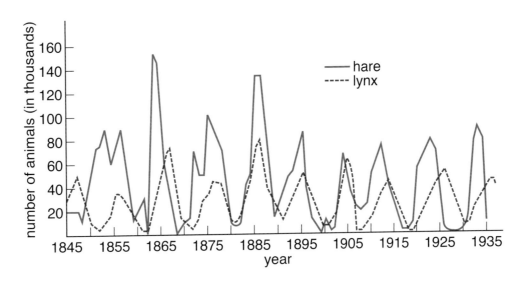

Figure 1

Size of lynx and hare populations, 1845–1935

Canadian lynx, shown in Figure 2, are almost entirely dependent on snowshoe hares as food. The lynx is a medium-size cat that resembles a bobcat, but has longer legs. The lynx ranges throughout Canada and 14 northern states including Washington, Oregon, Wisconsin, and New York. These secretive animals prefer old growth forests that have plenty of downed trees, which serve as hiding places.

Figure 2

Canadian lynx

The snowshoe hare (Figure 3) is so named because of its large hind feet that keep it from sinking in the snow. The white hair of a snowshoe in winter morphs to mottled brown in the summer, helping the animal blend with its surroundings in every season. Throughout the year, the hare has distinguishing tufts of black fur at the tips of its ears. The ears of snowshoes are not as long as many other rabbits, an adaptation that prevents the loss of body heat. In this experiment, you will find out how changes in the sizes of snowshoe hare populations affect the population sizes of Canadian lynx.

winter   summer

Figure 3

Snowshoe hare

Time Required

55 minutes

Materials

- ➥ 6 index cards
- ➥ small box of toothpicks
- ➥ graph paper
- ➥ colored pencils
- ➥ science notebook

> **Safety Note**   Please review and follow the safety guidelines at the beginning of this volume.

Procedure

1. In this experiment, toothpicks represent hares and squares cut from index cards represent lynx.

2. Use scissors to cut an index card into 20 squares (lynx).

3. Your desktop will serve as the habitat for hares and lynx. Randomly distribute six hares (toothpicks) on your desktop. Copy the data table in your science notebook. Allow space for adding more rows. The starting numbers of hares and lynx are listed on the data table.

4. The first round of this experiment will begin with one lynx. With your eyes closed, toss a lynx onto your desk.

   a. If the card strikes a hare, then the hare is eaten by the lynx. As a result, the lynx survives and has one offspring. To show this, remove one toothpick. Pick up the existing lynx card and a second card to represent the offspring. All of the hares that are left on your desktop reproduce and have two offspring. Show this by adding two toothpicks for each existing toothpick

   b. If the card does not strike a hare, then the lynx does not survive or reproduce. Put the lynx card back in the stack. All of the hares reproduce and have two offspring. Show this by adding two new toothpicks for each existing toothpick.

Record the number of hares and lynx at the end of round 1 on the data table on the row titled "Round 1."

5. Close your eyes and toss the lynx card (or cards) on the desktop. Follow the same rules: if a lynx touches a hare, the lynx reproduces and the hare dies. All hares that are not touched by a lynx have two offspring. Record the numbers of hares and lynx on the data table.

6. Continue step 5 for a total of 10 rounds. Cut index cards as needed to keep up your supply of lynx.

7. Graph the data collected on the data table. Show rounds (which represent time) on the X-axis and number of organisms on the Y-axis. Use two different colors for lynx and hares.

Data Table		
	Hares	**Lynx**
Start	6	1
Round 1		
Round 2		
Round 3		

Analysis

1. Examine Figure 1, which shows the sizes of lynx and hare populations from 1845 to 1935. Answer the following questions.

   a. What was the population of lynx in 1845?

   b. What was the population of hare that same year?

   c. What was the population of lynx in 1852?

   d. What was the population of hares that same year?

   e. Generally speaking, is the hare population highest when the lynx population is large or small?

2. In your experiment, when the population of hares was low, did the lynx always find food? Explain your answer.

3. In your experiment, how did the size of the predator population affect the prey population?

4. Based on your experimental results, define *predator-prey cycle*.

What's Going On?

Traditionally, predator-prey relationships deal with a carnivorous species that feeds on a herbivorous one. However, the relationship also holds for herbivores feeding on producers or parasites and their hosts. Over a long period of time, the predator's population size follows that of the prey. So if the prey population size decreases, so does the population of the predator. There is always a time lag between the predator's response to the prey's changes, so the cycle is not exactly in phase.

Predators do not always depend on only one prey species. If they did, the predators might completely consume that species, then starve to death. Most often, several types of organisms serve as prey for animals near the top of the food chain. In nature, lynx are known to feed on mice, voles, and birds if hares are not available.

Connections

Predator and prey populations are usually stable, despite their cyclic fluctuations. The value of balanced predator-prey relationships becomes evident when the prey no longer have any predators. This has happened in many instances, and usually at the hands of humans. In 1788, colonists entering the continent of Australia brought caged rabbits with them. These animals were raised for food. The rabbits were kept in enclosures around homes and barns. Some escaped, but their populations were kept in check by native predators. Over time, these predators were hunted to extinction, leaving the rabbits free to range as they pleased. Today, rabbits are a serious problem in Australia. They are responsible for the loss of hundreds of species of plants, including trees. By eating groundcover plants, the animals expose soil to erosion by wind and rain. Loss of topsoil has damaged the landscape, making it impossible to replace native vegetation.

 Want to Know More?

See appendix for Our Findings.

Further Reading

DeRoos, J. Barry. "Introduction to the Predator-Prey Problem," January 9, 2002. Available online. URL: http://home.messiah.edu/~deroos/ CSC171/PredPrey/PPIntro.htm. This Web site includes a simulation that shows how changes in one population affects the other.

Science Daily. *Predator-Prey Interactions Are Key 'Conductors' Of Nature's Synchronicity,* July 23, 2009. Available online. URL: http://www. sciencedaily.com/releases/2009/07/090722142830.htm. Accessed August 9, 2009. The article discusses the newest research on factors that influence predator-prey cycle.

University of Michigan. Introduction to Global Change, "Predation and Parasitism." Available online. URL: http://www.globalchange.umich. edu/globalchange1/current/lectures/predation/predation.html. Accessed August 8, 2009. This lecture from the Global Change program at the University of Michigan discusses changes in predator and prey populations.

10. What Are the Stages of Ecological Succession?

Topic

Stages of ecological succession can be identified on or near the school campus.

Introduction

Have you ever taken a stroll along a nature trail? The area in which the trail was built is probably under protection from development. As you look around a nature trail, you can see a natural community of plants and animals. Try to imagine what this area looked like 100 years ago. What events could have caused the changes that this area has experienced over the last century? What do you think the area will be like in another 100 years?

All communities undergo changes because of variations in the availability of resources. Each species of plants in an area competes with other species for nutrients, water, space, and sunlight. The first plants to move into an available space, the *pioneers*, are usually small. As the plants grow and spread, they change the environment. Their roots reach into rocky soil and help break it apart, making the area more hospitable to other plants. When taller plants move in, they produce shade and consume nutrients and water, eventually crowding out the pioneers. Over time, trees may appear, reducing the light availability even further and suppressing the growth of tall plants. As the plant life in a community shifts, so does the animal life. Very few animals can eat pioneer plants species. However, the arrival of tall plants offers leaves and seeds that feed a greater variety of organisms. When trees make their appearance and tall plants die out, the animal populations undergo further change. Eventually, a community reaches a steady state with the environment, becomes stable, and no longer undergoes changes. This point is known as the *climax community*. Most climax communities contain a wide diversity of plants and animals that exist in complex food chains.

The changes or succession of organisms in a community occur over a long period of time. Succession occurs in two ways. If an area is disturbed, *secondary succession* occurs. For example, a farmer might retire and stop plowing the fields every year. In a short time, plants will move into the fields. Weeds will come first, then young trees or shrubs will appear. Over a period of 20 years or more, a young forest may develop. The same kind of changes can be seen if a fire or tornado wipes out a natural community.

Primary succession occurs at a site that has never been colonized by living things. When a volcano erupts, hot lava flows out the top and down the side. When the lava cools, primary succession begins. Primary succession can also take place on sand dunes. On beaches, dunes are constantly being built and torn down by wind. When a new dune is created, grasses and other pioneer plants move in. The roots of beach grasses are deep, holding the sand in place and creating a stable environment for other plants. In a similar way, primary succession can be seen on soil that is deposited after a flood. *Alluvial* soil that is left by rising rivers is usually rich in nutrients. Seeds from nearby plants blow in and germinate on the rich, moist soil. In a short time, small trees establish a foothold and create an environment that attracts other organisms.

In this experiment, you will look for signs of secondary succession on or near the school campus. You will use the evidence you find to predict the future successional changes that will occur on the campus.

Time Required

55 minutes

Materials

- digital camera (optional)
- access to an outdoor area
- science notebook

Safety Note   Please review and follow the safety guidelines at the beginning of this volume.

Procedure

1. Take your science notebook, digital camera, and a pen or pencil and follow your teacher on an outdoor walk.

2. At the first stop along the walk, look for signs of succession. For example, if you are in a parking lot, are there any cracks where tiny plants have started growing? Along the edges, is the pavement crumbling? In a field, vacant lot, or park, are any young trees sprouting? Record the signs of succession in your science notebook by either sketching the site or by photographing it with a digital camera.

3. Visit at least 10 sites with your teacher.

4. Return to the classroom and analyze your sketches, notes, or photographs. Select one of the sites. For this site, draw what you think the area will look like:

   a. 20 years from now,

   b. 60 years from now,

   c. 100 years from now.

   For the purposes of your drawing, assume that the area is not disrupted by humans or by forces of nature.

Analysis

1. In your own words, define *succession*.

2. Explain the difference between primary and secondary succession.

3. Indicate what type of succession will occur in each of the following examples. Use "P" for primary succession and "S" for secondary succession.

   _____ A volcanic eruption forms a new island in the Pacific Ocean.

   _____ Fire destroys a forest.

   _____ A central city park is abandoned.

   _____ After a hurricane, new sand dunes are created behind existing dunes.

   _____ A paved street is rarely used.

4. How do humans impact natural succession?

5. Plants colonize an area before animals. Why do you think this is so?

6. Examine Figure 1. Explain what is happening in each frame of the figure.

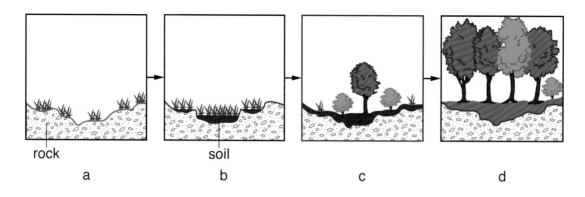

rock

soil

a   b   c   d

Figure 1

7. The data table shows succession that has occurred at a location in Wisconsin. Use the data table to help you answer questions a through e.

Data Table	
Stage of Succession	**Dominant Plants**
a	None (The land has recently been cleared by a bulldozer.)
b	Annual grasses
c	Several types of shrubs
d	Small trees
e	Large trees

a. What is the pioneer species?

b. What plants are found in the climax community?

c. In which stages of succession were the plants exposed to full sunlight?

d. Why are light-loving grasses not found in a stage e community?

8. Number the pictures in Figure 2 from 1 through 4 to show the correct order of succession.

Figure 2

What's Going On?

Unless your school is situated near a beach, creek, or river, all of the outdoor areas you visited on campus showed signs of secondary succession. On your outdoor walk, you probably saw weeds invading lawns, flower beds, or cracks in sidewalks. The term *weed* is applied to any unwanted plant species. However, these plants play important roles in succession. Weeds are very successful early invaders for several reasons. These plants produce a lot of seeds that are distributed by wind. In addition, they can thrive in less-than-optimal environments because they get all the nutrients they need from the abiotic aspects of the soil. In addition, weeds grow quickly, are relatively small, and have short life cycles. Weeds are replaced by woody species of plants that grow slowly and are long-lived.

When weeds die, their biomass becomes part of the organic matter of the soil. Weeds are replaced by small, woody shrubs whose seeds are heavy and are usually dispersed by animals or by gravity. These woody plants thrive on the organic matter left in the soil by earlier weeds. Woody shrubs live longer than weeds and create an environment that can support larger plants such as trees.

Connections

The transformation of a pond or lake to a terrestrial community is a form of primary succession known as *aquatic succession*. A young pond like the one in Figure 3, has a bare bottom and plenty of open water. In time, *plankton,* one-celled organisms that float in the upper water column, take up residence. These tiny animals and plantlike creatures provide food for insects and small fish. At the same time, sediment washes into the pond and forms a rich layer that can support rooted water plants. The roots of water plants hold the bottom layers in place and help build up dead plant and animal matter. As sediment and organic matter accumulates, the pond becomes shallower. Plants prefer shallow water to deep because of the availability of sunlight, so more plants make their homes in the pond. Over time, the water becomes richer in nutrients, and plants grow across the surface. Eventually the shallow pond develops into a *marsh*. Sediments and organic matter continue to collect, until finally the soil emerges above the waterline. Grasses take root in the soil and a meadow develops. Depending on the climate, the meadow may evolve into a prairie or forest (see Figure 3, which shows changes that occur over 40 years).

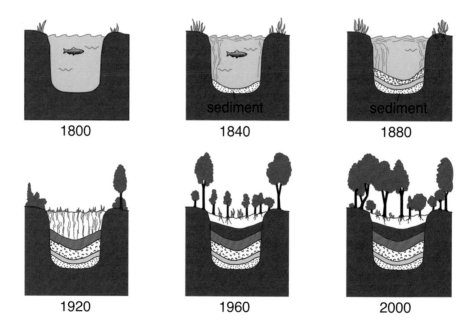

Figure 3

From 1800 to 2000, a pond changes to a terrestrial community.

Want to Know More?

See appendix for Our Findings.

Further Reading

"Ecological Succession." The Virtual Nature Trail at Penn State New Kensington, July 12, 2009. Available online. URL: http://www.psu.edu/dept/nkbiology/naturetrail/succession.htm. Accessed January 2, 2010. This Web site discusses succession along a Penn State nature trail.

Simonis, Joe. "Plant Succession on Coastal Sand Dunes." University of Illinois. Available online. URL: http://www.life.illinois.edu/cheeseman/ib447/MichiganPPT/DuneSuccession.ppt. Accessed August 15, 2009. Simonis provides beautiful photographs of sand dune succession in a PowerPoint presentation.

State of Michigan, Department of Natural Resources. "Succession: Changing Land, Changing Wildlife," 2003. Available online. URL: http://www.michigandnr.com/publications/pdfs/wildlife/viewingguide/eco_succession.htm. Accessed August 15, 2009. This Web site explains how farmland has developed into forests.

11. Observing Plant Growth in Different Biomes

Topic

Plants experience diverse challenges to survival in different biomes.

Introduction

A *biome* is a large geographic area that has a characteristic climate and is home to a distinct set of plants and animals. The distribution of biomes around the world is dependent on the climate at each location. Climate refers to the weather conditions of a region over a long period of time. Figure 1 shows the distribution of biomes around the world.

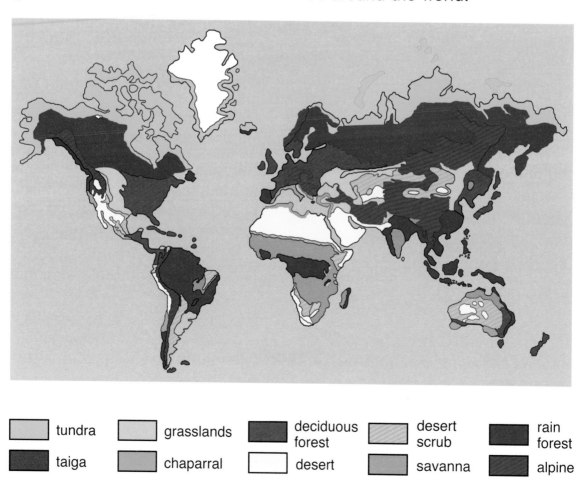

tundra	grasslands	deciduous forest	desert scrub	rain forest
taiga	chaparral	desert	savanna	alpine

Figure 1

Two determining factors of climate are temperature and amount of *precipitation*. Both factors are influenced by the Earth's spherical shape and the tilt of its axis, characteristics that affect the amount of solar energy reaching the planet's surface. The spherical shape of Earth means that more sunlight hits the areas around the equator than the poles. Therefore, the climate of the tropics is warmer than the climate of the poles. The Earth's tilt accounts for seasonal variations in the amount of sunlight an area receives, as shown in Figure 2:

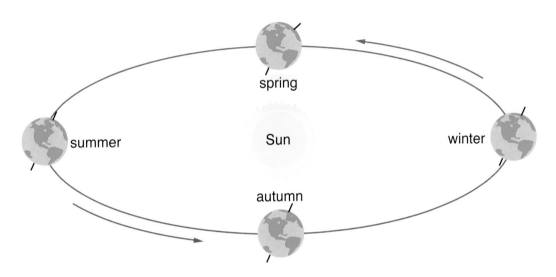

Figure 2

Seasons on Earth are due to the tilt of Earth on its axis.

The amount of precipitation is important because water supports life. In regions where precipitation is abundant, plant growth is profuse and productivity is high. As a result, the region can support a large variety and number of animals. Precipitation is relatively low at 30 degrees north (°N) and 30°S *latitudes*. It is also low at the interior regions of continents because they are so far from the ocean, which is the source of moisture. Precipitation is higher in regions where warm, moist air rises then cools, releasing its moisture. This weather pattern is common near the equator and is responsible for the tropical rain forests.

Temperature is a key factor in ecosystems because most organisms can only survive within a narrow range of temperatures. Plants, for example, cannot survive in regions that are too cold or too hot for them. As a general rule, warm temperatures lead to high plant productivity. Temperature is affected by both latitude and elevation. The highest temperatures are found near the equator where there are no seasons.

Temperatures are lower at latitudes north or south of the equator. In these temperate regions, seasons occur. Mountainous areas are cooler than flat ones because temperature decreases with altitude. An increase of 3,280 feet (1,000 meters [m]) in elevation reduces temperatures by about 43.7 degrees Fahrenheit (°F) (6.5 degrees Celsius [°C]).

In this experiment, you and your classmates will raise three different kinds of plants under conditions similar to those found in two of the major biomes. By doing so, you can determine how the amounts of available sunlight and precipitation affect plant growth.

Time Required

55 minutes for day 1
up to 20 minutes a day on follow-up days for 2 weeks

Materials

- ◦◇ books on biomes or access to the Internet
- ◦◇ 2 medium-sized flower pots
- ◦◇ access to potting soil
- ◦◇ access to sandy soil
- ◦◇ access to manure
- ◦◇ access to clay soil
- ◦◇ access to water
- ◦◇ watering can or beaker
- ◦◇ ruler
- ◦◇ 5 lima bean seeds
- ◦◇ 5 corn seeds
- ◦◇ 20 radish seeds
- ◦◇ lamp, grow light, or access to a window
- ◦◇ timer for lamp
- ◦◇ 4 labels
- ◦◇ waterproof pen
- ◦◇ science notebook

| Safety Note | Please review and follow the safety guidelines at the beginning of this volume. |

Procedure, Part 1

1. Your teacher will assign you two biomes. Research these biomes in the books provided or on the Internet to find:

    a. the soil type,

    b. the average amount of rain per year (and convert that to rain per day),

    c. the amount of light that reaches small plants,

    d. the average temperature.

2. Label the flower pots with the names of the biomes you were assigned.

3. Fill the pots with soil, leaving a space of about 2 inches (in.) (5 centimeters [cm]) at the top. In each pot, use the combination of soils that is most like the biomes assigned to you.

4. Germinate some seeds for the experiment. To do so:

    a. In each pot, plant five lima bean seeds and five corn seeds at a depth of about 1 in. (2.5 cm) Spread the 20 radish seeds across the soil, then gently press them into the soil. Radish seeds should not be planted deeply

    b. Water the seeds in both pots until the soil is damp, but water is not standing.

    c. Place each pot in a well-lit area.

Procedure, Follow-up Days

1. Observe the plants for 3 or 4 days. Watch for tiny, folded leaves emerging from the soil. If the soil becomes dry to the touch. add water.

2. After the seeds have germinated and the corn and beans are 2 or 3 in. (5 to 7 cm) tall, begin the experiment. Provide water and light to each pot according to the research you did on the biomes. For example, if one of your pots is labeled "desert," it will receive only a fraction of an inch of water during the entire experimental period. On the other hand, a pot labeled "rain forest" will receive about 0.2

in. (1 cm) of water each day. In addition, the desert pot will receive direct light all day while the rain forest pot will only receive a few hours of indirect light. Sunlight can be provided by a lamp, a grow light, or a window.

3. Every other day for 2 weeks observe the plants in your two biomes. Use a ruler to measure the heights of all of the bean seedlings. Average the measurements. Copy two data tables like the one below in your science notebook, one for each biome. Record the averages on the data tables. Do the same for the corn seedlings and the radish seedlings. Extend your data tables if necessary to accommodate all the data.

4. After you water the plants, take notes of the color and condition of your seedlings. Record your findings in the last columns of the data tables under "Notes on color and condition of plants."

5. Visit the other lab groups and take notes about the plants in their pots.

Data Table				
Date	Average height of bean seedlings	Average height of corn seedlings	Average height of radish seedling	Notes on color and condition of plants

Analysis

1. In your own words, define *biome*.
2. How did you regulate the amount of light your biomes received?

3. In which biome pot did plants grow the taller? Why do you think this is so?

4. Did all three types of plants grow equally well in the pot in which the plants grew taller?

5. In which biome pot were plants greener? Why do you think this is so?

6. Did all three types of plants grow equally well in the pot in which the plants were greener?

7. In this experiment, the tundra and taiga were not included. How do you think the plants would have grown in these biomes?

8. Why did the plants grow differently in each biome pot?

What's Going On?

In this experiment, you grew three types of plants under different conditions to see how they fared. The conditions you established mimicked those in two of the major biomes. By carrying out this experiment, you can see some of the stresses placed on plants by availability of light and water.

Plants have special adaptations for the biomes in which they live. In the tropical rain forest, plants receive about 80 in. (203 cm) of rain each year. This much water, and the humidity associated with it, could cause the growth of molds and bacteria on the plants. As a result, rainforest plants have *adaptations* to shed water. Some have oily leaves that help the water roll off. Other have leaves with drip tips or grooves to remove water.

Rainforest plants have other unique adaptations for their environment. Sunlight levels are low on the rainforest floor, so plants are adapted to take advantage of every bit of Sun available. Many have stalks that rotate to follow the Sun's journey across the sky. Others possess very large leaves to help them collect light. Plants called *epiphytes* grow on top of other plants, getting a leg up toward the Sun. Plants that live in the upper layer or *canopy* of the rain forest have small, leathery leaves to reduce water loss. Another plant adaptation is the development of special supports near the base called *buttresses*, thick ridges to help hold up tall trees in the thin rainforest soil.

Desert plants, which live in a sunny, hot, dry climate, have their own adaptations. Most can store water in their tissues. In addition, the leaves of desert plants are designed to conserve water rather than lose it. Some leaves, like those in the cactus in Figure 3, are small and coated with wax to prevent water loss. Desert plants also grow very long, deep roots that explore for water down to the water table. Flowers only appear in the desert after a rain, and last for just a short time to avoid water loss.

Figure 3

**Desert plants such as cacti have small, waxy leaves
and spines to conserve moisture.**

Connections

Just like plants, the animals that live in each biome show adaptations for their environments. In the desert, many animals do not drink water. Instead, they get all of the water they need from their food. To stay cool during the day, animals bury beneath the sand or sleep in shady places. At twilight, when temperatures are lower, the *crepuscular* animals such as snakes and Gila monsters come out to look for food. *Nocturnal* animals take advantage of the cool of night by waiting until after the Sun sets to hunt their food. This group includes bats, many other mammals, and some reptiles.

Rain forest organisms also show special adaptations. This biome supports a tremendous number of animals, so there is a lot of competition for food. Many animals sport camouflage that helps them blend in with the environment, an advantage for both predators and prey.

Other animals are poisonous. To warn predators of their deadly toxins, they are brightly colored. The poison arrow toad (Figure 4) exudes a chemical on its skin that is toxic to all that consume it. Predators quickly learn to avoid animals with its bright coloration.

Figure 4

The bright colors of poison arrow toads warn of its toxicity.

Want to Know More?

See appendix for Our Findings.

Further Reading

Missouir Botanical Garden. "What's It Like Where You Live?" 2005. Available online. URL: http://www.mbgnet.net/. Accessed August 17, 2009. The Missouri Botanical Garden provides information on both terrestrial and aquatic biomes on its Web site.

Pidwirny, Michael. "Terrestrial Biome," December 4, 2007. *Encyclopedia of the Earth*. Available online. URL: http://www.eoearth.org/article/ Terrestrial_biome. Accessed August 17, 2009. Pidwirny discusses the role of natural selection in development of the species that inhabit various biomes.

University of California Museum of Paleontology. "The World's Biomes." Available online. URL: http://www.ucmp.berkeley.edu/exhibits/biomes/ index.php. Accessed September 1, 2009. This Web site describes both terrestrial and aquatic ecosystems.

12. Energy in Ecosystems

Topic
Temperatures in ecosystems vary depending on plant cover.

Introduction
The Sun is the source of almost all of the energy that supports living things. When sunlight strikes the Earth, it may be absorbed, scattered, or reflected. The reflected radiation is in the form of heat. Although the same amount of energy hits all the ecosystems within an area, the amount of reflected radiation varies depending on soil, water, and plant life. As a result, temperatures in neighboring ecosystems can vary.

Heat energy due to reflected radiation is one of several essential *abiotic*, or nonliving, factors in an ecosystem. All of the abiotic factors in an environment affect the living, or *biotic*, parts. In a similar way, the living parts of an ecosystem affect the abiotic factors. In this experiment, you will develop a hypothesis about how the amount of plant life in an ecosystem affects the area's temperature. Then you will develop an experiment to see if your hypothesis is correct.

Time Required
65 minutes

Materials
- meterstick
- thermometer
- bucket
- soil

- lamp
- access to 3 or more outdoor locations that vary in amount of vegetation
- science notebook

Safety Note Please review and follow the safety guidelines at the beginning of this volume.

Procedure

1. Answer Analysis questions 1 through 3.

2. Your job is to develop a hypothesis about how the presence of vegetation affects air temperature in an ecosystem. Vegetation refers to plants, and it includes grass, shrubs, and trees.

3. Write your hypothesis on the data table.

4. Design an experiment to test your hypothesis. You can use any of the supplies provided by your teacher, but you may not need to use all of them. Before you begin work on your experiment, decide exactly what you are going to do. Keep this point in mind: Your experiment should include only one *variable*—the amount of vegetation. Control for all other factors. For example, in each of the location where you plan to measure temperature, you should do so at the same time of day and at the same distance above the ground.

5. Write the steps you plan to take (your experimental procedure) and the materials you plan to use (materials list) on the data table below. Show your procedure and materials list to the teacher. If you get teacher approval, proceed with your experiment. If not, modify your work and show it to your teacher again.

6. Once you have teacher approval, assemble the materials you need and begin your procedure.

7. Collect your results on a data table of your own design.

8. Answer the rest of the Analysis questions.

Data Table	
Your hypothesis	
Your experimental procedure	
Your materials list	
Teacher's approval	

Analysis

1. Why is the air just above the Earth's surface warm?

2. What kind of surface would you expect to reflect the most heat energy: smooth, unvegetated surface or a surface covered with plants? Explain your reasoning.

3. Temperature is only one abiotic factor in an ecosystem. What are some others?

4. Describe the ecosystems involved in your experiment.

5. Based on the data you collected, how does vegetation affect the temperature of an ecosystem?

6. When people move into ecosystems, they often change the number and types of plants. How do you think removing vegetation to build homes affects the temperature of an ecosystem?

What's Going On?

In this experiment, you developed your own procedure for finding out how vegetation affects the temperature of an ecosystem. To carry out an experiment successfully, you first developed a testable hypothesis. As you set up your experiment, you also had to control for variables. The only variable to be tested in this experiment is the effect of vegetation on temperature. You had to control other variables such as time of day, position of the thermometer in each ecosystem, and exposure to wind.

Scientists have learned that bare land reflects more heat into the atmosphere than land that is covered in plants. When soil is covered with plants, some of the Sun's energy is absorbed by the plants and used for biological processes, thus reducing the amount of energy reflected. If the soil is covered with small bushes and shrubs, even more of the Sun's energy is used by the plants, further reducing the amount reflected. Forests take up even more heat than shrubs and bushes (see Figure 1).

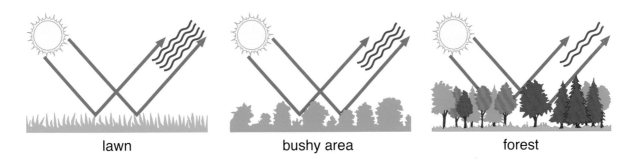

lawn   bushy area   forest

Figure 1

Connections

Changes in land use seem to be affecting temperatures on Earth's surface in two ways: through surface reflection and through exchange of heat between the air and the surface. Earth's *albedo*, or surface reflection, directly influences the climate of a region. Practices that increase albedo also decrease surface temperature. For examples, the replacement of forests with farms or pastures in the *middle latitudes*, the Earth's temperate zones, has lead to an increase in albedo. As a result, the amount of the Sun's energy reflected into the atmosphere has increased and surface temperatures have dropped.

On the other hand, plants increase the amount of water entering the air. Plants take up water from the soil through their roots. This water travels through the stems to the leaves, from which it is released through microscopic holes called *stomata* in the process of *transpiration*, which releases heat (see Figure 2). The roles of these two processes influencing climate depend on seasons. From fall until spring, the albedo effect has the most influence on climate. In the summer, when plants abound, transpiration plays a more important role in influencing climate.

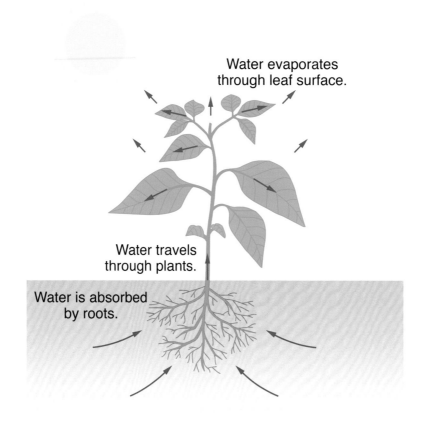

Water evaporates
through leaf surface.

Water travels
through plants.

Water is absorbed
by roots.

Figure 2

Want to Know More?

See appendix for Our Findings.

Further Reading

Lindsey, Rebecca. "Climate and Earth's Energy Budget," July 14, 2008. NASA. Available online. URL: http://earthobservatory.nasa.gov/Features/EnergyBalance/. Accessed September 6, 2009. Lindsey explains how solar radiation is absorbed and used on the Earth's surface.

NASA. "Why Isn't Earth Hot As An Oven." Available online. URL: http://terra.nasa.gov/FactSheets/EnergyBalance/. Accessed September 12, 2009. Despite the incredible amount of solar energy striking Earth, the surface does not overheat. This Web site explains what happens to the Sun's energy on Earth.

"Sun, Earth, and Temperature Change," 2009. Schlumberger Excellence in Educational Development. Available online. URL: http://www.seed.slb.com/subcontent.aspx?id=4070. Accessed September 12, 2009. This Web site explain several factors that influence temperatures on Earth's surface.

13. The Role of Decomposers in the Nitrogen Cycle

Topic

Plants are able to extract nitrogen from decomposed leaves.

Introduction

Nitrogen (N) is an essential element for living things. Cells require nitrogen to make two types of organic compounds: proteins and nucleic acids. Nitrogen gas (N_2) is abundant in the air, making up 79 percent of the atmosphere. However, living things are unable to take up and use nitrogen gas directly. Plants get their nitrogen from the soil after it has been "fixed," or converted into nitrogen compounds or *ions*, charged particles. Three important forms of nitrogen are *urea* ($(NH_2)_2CO$, *ammonia* (NH_3), and nitrate ions (NO_3^-). Animals are able to get nitrogen by eating plants or animals that have consumed plants.

Nitrogen that is tied up in the bodies of plants and animals is eventually returned to the soil. When plants and animals die, the proteins in their tissues decompose and the nitrogen compounds are released into the environment. In addition, the *excrement* of animals contains nitrogen compounds. Microorganisms convert these nitrogen compounds into ammonia, which can once again be taken up by plants. In the soil, other organisms, known as *nitrifying bacteria*, change some of the ammonia into nitrate ions, which plants can easily absorb. In this way, nitrogen travels in a cycle from the soil, to plants, to animals, and back to the soil (see Figure 1). In this experiment, you will compare plant growth in soil that contains decomposed plant matter and soil that does not.

Time Required

55 minutes on day 1
20 minutes on each follow up day for a period of 1 to 2 weeks

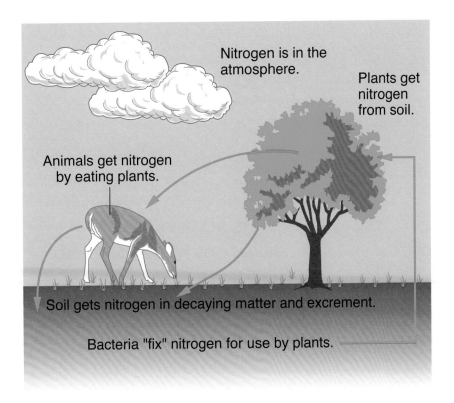

Figure 1

Materials

- sand (about 10 cups)
- decayed leaves
- 8 corn or bean seedlings
- 2 medium-size flowerpots
- grow light or access to a sunny window
- access to water
- ruler
- science notebook

Safety Note   Please review and follow the safety guidelines at the beginning of this volume.

Procedure

1. Your job is to design and perform an experiment to find out whether plants grow as well in soil that contains crushed, dead leaves as they do in soil that contains decayed leaves. The soil you will use in this experiment is sand. To begin your experiment, select a hypothesis:

    a. Plants grow better in soil that contains decayed leaves.

    b. Plants grow better in soil that contains crushed leaves.

    Write your hypothesis on the data table.

2. For this experiment, decide how you will define "better." Better could refer to height, so plants that grow "better" would be those that are taller. Or, better could refer to color. If this is the case, plants that grow "better" would be darker green. Better could also refer to the diameter of the stem, number of leaves on the plant, or the size of plant leaves. Add your definition of "better" in your hypothesis.

3. Develop an experimental procedure, a plan of what you are going to do. Write the steps you plan to take (your experimental procedure) and the materials you plan to use (materials list) on the data table on page 87. Show your procedure and materials list to the teacher. If you get teacher approval, proceed with your experiment. If not, modify your work and show it to your teacher again. Keep these points in mind:

    a. Your experiment should test only one variable, the effect of decayed leaves on the growth of plants.

    b. All other variables should be constant. For example, all plants must receive the same amount of light and be kept at the same temperature.

4. Once you have teacher approval, assemble the materials you need and begin your procedure.

5. Collect your results on a data table of your own design.

Analysis

1. How is nitrogen released from the tissues of dead plants and animals?

2. Based on your experimental results, was your hypothesis correct? Explain your reasoning.

Data Table	
Your hypothesis	
Your experimental procedure	
Your materials list	
Teacher's approval	

3. What is the difference between a dead leaf and a decayed leaf?

4. A good experiment tests only one variable. In this experiment, what was the variable?

5. What are some variables that you controlled in your experiment?

6. Why is it essential that you control variables in an experiment?

What's Going On?

In this experiment, you compared how well plants grow in soil that contains decayed leaves to how well they grow in soil without them. Decayed leaves have undergone the process of decomposition. As a result, the nitrogen in those leaves has been freed of the plant tissues and is available to be used again. The seedlings that you raised in soil with decayed leaves had access to nitrogen, whereas those in soil without decayed leaves did not.

Plants living in nitrogen-rich soil are greener, stouter, and taller than those in soil that is nitrogen poor. Nitrogen is a component of many essential molecules, including proteins. The protein that makes plants green is *chlorophyll*, a green pigment (see Figure 2). Chlorophyll is the site of *photosynthesis*, the process in which water and carbon dioxide are converted into glucose and oxygen in the presence of sunlight. Other proteins in plants have structural roles, and are used to build plant tissue. In addition, *adenosine triphosphate (ATP)*, an energy carrying molecule, contains nitrogen. Without ATP, plant cells cannot carry out any chemical processes.

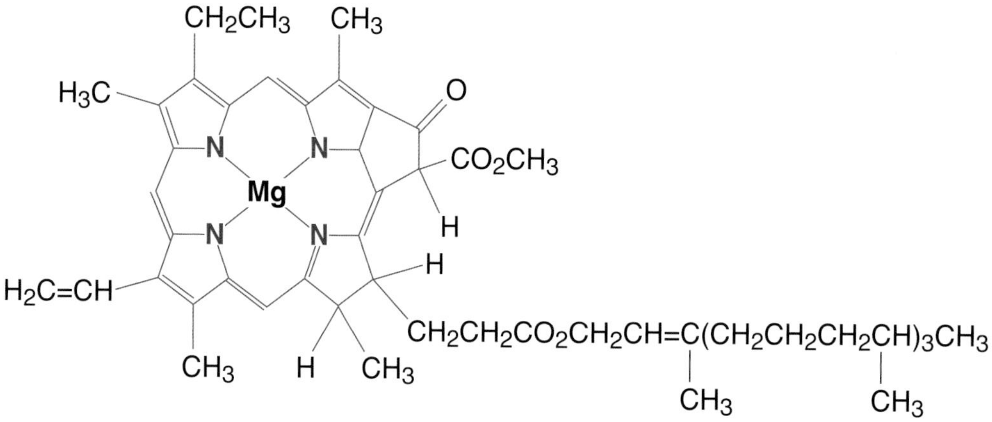

Figure 2

The structural formula of chlorophyll

Connections

Nitrogen enters the environment from several sources. The process of decomposition is a chemical process that releases nitrogen from excreta and tissues and returns it to the environment. Nitrifying bacteria can also add the compound to the environment. Many of these simple organisms live in *symbiotic* relationships with *legumes*, a group of plants that include several types of beans. Another source of nitrogen in the environment is lightning. The energy of lightning breaks the chemical bonds in nitrogen gas, enabling nitrogen to react to oxygen and forming nitrogen oxides.

When the oxides dissolve in rainwater, they form nitrates that enter the soil and are available to plant roots.

Chemical processes also remove nitrogen from the environment and return it to the air. In *denitrification*, nitrogen compounds are converted into nitrogen gas, which enters the air. Some denitrification is carried out by *anaerobes*, bacteria that live in the soil where oxygen is not available. In this way, nitrogen cycles between the atmosphere and the environment. For eons, this cycle has been a balanced one, but a shift is occurring. Humans are converting nitrogen gas into fertilizers to use on crops. As a result, they are upsetting the balance of the natural nitrogen cycle, putting more nitrogen into the environment than nature can remove. Figure 3 shows how much nitrogen is fixed naturally as well as the nitrogen fixed in man-made fertilizers and through burning fossil fuels worldwide.

Nitrogen enrichment in ecosystems can cause problems. For example, excess nitrogen in waterways causes *algal blooms*, rapid growth of algae that clogs channels and supports oxygen-consuming bacteria. As a result, an algal bloom can lead to loss of oxygen in an aquatic environment as well as the organisms that depend on oygen.

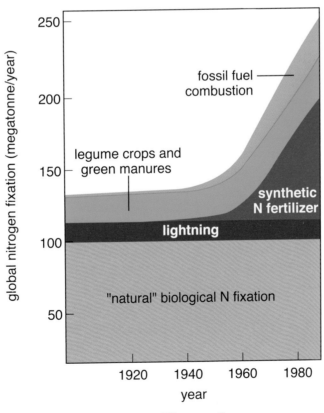

Figure 3

The amount of nitrogen gas converted to nitrogen compound each year

Want to Know More?

See appendix for Our Findings.

Further Reading

Elevitch, Craig, and Kim Wilkinson. "Nitrogen Fixing Trees: Multipurpose Pioneers," August 25, 2009. agroforestry.net. Available online. URL: http://www.agroforestry.net/pubs/NFTs.html. Accessed September 6, 2009. Some trees are able to fix nitrogen. This article discusses the role of the trees in tropical and subtropical regions.

Mapes, Lynda V. "Rivers, Sewage-Treatment Plants Carry Nitrogen to Sound," 2009. *Seattle Times*. Available online. URL: http://seattletimes. nwsource.com/html/localnews/2008682957_pugetsound29m.html. Accessed September 12, 2009. Like many cities, Puget Sound in Seattle, Washington, is polluted with nitrogen from sewage treatment plants. This article discusses the problem.

Specter, Christy. "How Does Your Garden Grow?" September 1, 2001. Soil Science Education. Available online. URL: http://soil.gsfc.nasa.gov/soilfert/npk.htm. Accessed September 5, 2009. Sponsored by NASA, the Soil Science Education Web site discusses soil nutrients and other aspects of soil fertility.

14. Invasive Species' Impact on an Ecosystem

Topic

The introduction of an invasive species to an ecosystem can be detrimental to native inhabitants.

Introduction

Populations, groups of the same kinds of individuals living in the same area at a given time, are always in a state of flux. New organisms are born or *migrate* into an area while other organisms die out or move out. Theoretically, a population will grow quickly as long as the environment can support its needs. But in the real world, environments cannot support constantly growing populations because resources are limited. As population density increases, resources become scarce. At that point, members of the population must compete with each other for food, water, light, shelter, and space. The factors or resources that influence the size of a population are called *limiting factors*.

In long-term, stable populations, there is a delicate balance among the organisms and the ecosystem. The introduction of a new species to an ecosystem can interrupt this balance and endanger the survival of the natives living there. A species that is not native to an area is called an *invasive species*. The introduction of wild rabbits to Australia created severe problems in Australian ecosystems.

British hunters and colonists brought wild, nonnative rabbits (see Figure 1) to Australia early in the 20th century. The rabbits reproduced quickly and began to consume large quantities of vegetation. The loss of vegetation threatened the survival of native animals that depended on plant life for food and shelter. The wild rabbits even consumed pasture grasses and shrubs so that livestock did not have adequate food. In addition, the rabbits dug holes that caused soil erosion, further reducing plant density. The Australian government estimates that damage caused by the wild rabbits has topped $500 million dollars.

Figure 1

Wild rabbits

The rabbit population in Australia grew out control because the introduced animal had no natural predators. Without predators to limit their population size, the number of rabbits grew out of control. Eventually humans had to intervene, releasing an antirabbit virus in the mid 20th century. The virus was initially successful in reducing rabbit populations, but the surviving rabbits have developed a resistance to the virus. The search continues for a way to undo the damage this invasive species caused. In this experiment, you will find out firsthand how an invasive species can change an ecosystem using a simulation.

Time Required

55 minutes

Materials

- green index card
- blue index card
- white index card
- yellow index card
- scissors
- marker
- science notebook

Procedure

1. Cut the green index card into 16 squares of about equal size. Use the marker to write the letter "P" on each square. This P stands for plants.

2. Cut the yellow card into 16 squares of about equal size. Use the marker to write the letter "S" for sheep on each square.

3. Cut the white index cards into 16 equal pieces. Write the letter "W" for wolf on each piece.

4. Cut the blue index card into 16 equal pieces. Write the letter "R" for rabbit on each piece.

5. You will be manipulating the paper squares in a simulation activity that spans several years. The plants, sheep, and wolves represent native species in this activity. The rabbits represent the invasive species. Follow these guidelines as you carry out the simulation.

    a. At the beginning of each year, the plants double in number.

    b. Each year, a sheep must consume one plant to survive to the next year.

    c. Each year, a wolf must consume two sheep to survive to the next year. The wolves are not predators of the rabbits.

    d. One sheep offspring is produced each year per every two surviving sheep.

    e. A pair of wolves produces two offspring every four years.

    f. Once the rabbits are introduced to the population, each pair will produce two offspring a year.

    g. Each year, a rabbit must consume one plant to survive to the next year.

    h. Each year the rabbits always eat their plants before the sheep begin to feed.

6. Your desktop represents an ecosystem. Organisms that are native to this ecosystem are plants, sheep, and wolves. In the original balanced ecosystem there are eight plants, eight sheep, and two wolves. Place these numbers of green, yellow, and white squares on your desk. This is the starting numbers for the population at the

beginning of the first year. Copy the data table and record these numbers on it under "Start" of Year 1.

7.   The year always begins by allowing the producers to reproduce first, so add eight more green cards to your desktop. (Refer to your guideline a through h as you complete year 1.) Allow the eight sheep to consume eight plants; remove eight green cards from the desktop. Allow the sheep to reproduce. Since you have four pair of sheep, you will have four offspring of sheep; add four yellow cards to the desktop. Next the predators must eat, so each of the two predators eats two sheep each; remove four yellow cards. The wolves do not reproduce until year four, so you do not have to adjust their numbers. Count the number of yellow, green, and white cards left on the desk and enter this number under "Finish" of Year 1.

8.   Continue this process, but in year 2 introduce two new rabbits to the desktop. Remember that rabbits eat before sheep and they produce two offspring for each pair. (Follow the rules a through h.) Record the starting and finishing numbers for year 2.

9.   Repeat the activity for years 3 and 4.

Data Table								
	Year 1		Year 2		Year 3		Year 4	
	Start	Finish	Start	Finish	Start	Finish	Start	Finish
Plants								
Sheep								
Wolves								
Rabbits								

Analysis

1. By the end of year 4, what happened to each of the four populations?

2. Before the rabbits were introduced, the population was relatively stable. Explain why.

3. What impact did the introduction of the rabbits have on the ecosystem?

4. Suppose you played the game again. If the number of plants tripled at the beginning of each year, would the results be different? Do you think the number of rabbits would eventually outnumber the sheep?

5. In the first half of the 20th century, kudzu, a fast-growing, hardy vine native to China, India, and Japan was introduced in the United States. Between 1930 and 1950, the Soil Conservation Corp supported the use of kudzu to control erosion. Why do you think that kudzu is now classified as an invasive species? Suggest problems that kudzu could cause.

What's Going On?

Ecosystems are composed of communities of organisms interacting in a certain environment. The introduction of a species that is not native to an area can disrupt the balance of an ecosystem. Even though the invasive species was not a threat to its original ecosystem, it can do great harm to a new ecosystem. In its native ecosystem, the population size was held in check by predators, parasites, and competition between species. When the invasive species is introduced to the new area, the controlling factors are no longer in place. Introduced species often reproduce very quickly due to lack of predators. As the new species increases in number, it competes for food, space, and water with the native species. Some of the native species may be forced to leave the area or die of starvation.

In the simulation, the balanced ecosystem consisted of plants (*producers*), sheep, and wolves. The sheep were plant eaters, *herbivores,* and the wolves were meat eaters, *carnivores*. This ecosystem was balanced so there was sufficient food for the sheep and the wolves without stripping the environment of its producers. In year two, another herbivore was introduced to the ecosystem. The rabbit was not native to the area and was considered an invasive species. The rabbit like the sheep, fed on producers. In head-to-head competition, the rabbits were superior to the sheep in obtaining their food first. The introduction of the rabbits to the ecosystem exhausted the number of producers in the ecosystem.

Connections

The introduction of invasive species is a global problem. You do not have to look far to see examples of invasive species that are changing ecosystems. For example, over the last 10 years, pet owners who have grown tired of keeping large snakes have dumped their Burmese pythons (see Figure 2) into the Everglades. Today, the python populations have grown significantly. These animals are considered invasive species and are disrupting the ecological balance of the Everglades. They are believed to be eating several endangered and threatened species of native Florida wildlife.

Figure 2

Burmese python

The Burmese python is just one of thousands of nonnative species in the United States. It costs billions of dollars annually to repair damage done by invasive species to crops, pastures, and waterways. Invasive species are thought to account for as much as 40 percent of species extinctions since the middle of the 18th century as these organisms compete with native species for food, space, water, and oxygen.

Want to Know More?

See appendix for Our Findings.

Further Reading

Austen, Jill. "Stopping a Burmese Python Invasion." The Nature Conservancy. Available online. URL: http://www.nature.org/wherewework/ northamerica/states/florida/science/art24101.html. Accessed September 7, 2009. Austen explains how snakes are damaging Everglade ecosystems and expanding their populations to the Florida Keys.

"Invasive Species." Available online. URL: http://www.youtube.com/ watch?v=-V5513w1XSk. Accessed September 7, 2009. In this video, Professor Anthony Ricciardi of McGill University and others explain how invasive species are transferred from their native environments to new locations.

U.S. Fish and Wildlife Service. "What Are Invasive Species?" August 14, 2009. Available online. URL: http://www.fws.gov/invasives/. Accessed September 7, 2009. This Web site describes invasive species, enables to you search by species, and provides suggestions for dealing with the problems caused by these organisms.

U.S. Geological Survey. "Welcome to the USGS Invasive Species Program," July 22, 2009. Available online. URL: http://biology.usgs. gov/invasive/. Accessed September 7, 2009. The Web site explains the problems caused by invasive organisms in the United States and has links to pages that discuss solutions to the problems.

15. Components of an Ecosystem

Topic

The parts of an ecosystem can be analyzed by observation.

Introduction

An *ecosystem* is a natural region made up of a *community* of living organisms interacting with their physical environment. The organisms within an ecosystem are linked by the transfer of energy and the sharing of nutrients. An ecosystem may be as large as a forest or prairie or as small as a mud puddle.

Both physical (*abiotic*) factors and living (*biotic*) factors make up an ecosystem. The primary abiotic components are energy from the Sun and inorganic materials, such as oxygen, water, and carbon dioxide. Biotic parts of the system include the plants, animals, fungi, and microorganisms that live there. Some of these living things are producers or *autotrophs*, organisms that can capture the Sun's energy and convert it to food. These are primarily plants but also include green algae and green bacteria. Others are consumers or *heterotrophs,* organisms that eat plants or other organisms. Decomposers like fungi and heterotrophic bacteria eventually break down the tissues of living things and return their minerals to the environment.

The driving force behind most food chains is the Sun's energy. This energy is passed from autotrophs to primary consumers, then on to secondary consumers. In the transfer, a lot of the energy is lost as heat. The series of organisms along which energy travels makes up a *food chain* (see Figure 1).

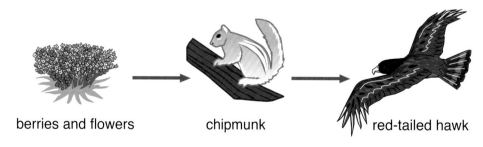

berries and flowers   chipmunk   red-tailed hawk

Figure 1

Food chain

In reality, feeding relationships are more complex than a food chain indicates. Several types of primary consumers may feed on the same plants. Food chains can be linked more realistically to explain relationships in an expanded diagram, a *food web* (see Figure 2). In this experiment, you will observe an ecosystem, identify the biotic and abiotic components, and develop a food web of the system.

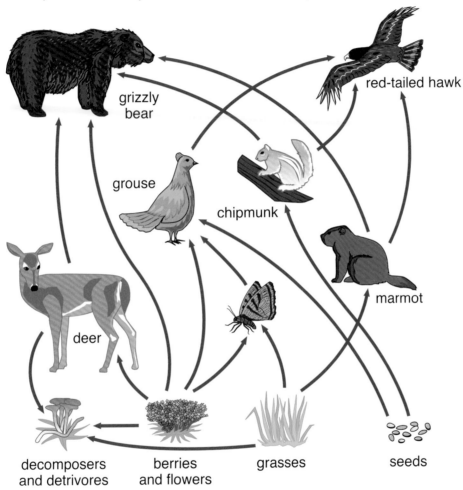

grizzly
bear

red-tailed hawk

grouse

chipmunk

marmot

deer

decomposers
and detrivores

berries
and flowers

grasses

seeds

Figure 2

Food web

Time Required

55 minutes

Materials

➠   towel (to sit on)

➠   clock or watch

⏩   access to an outdoor area

⏩   science notebook

Safety Note   Please review and follow the safety guidelines at the beginning of this volume.

Procedure

1. Copy the data table in your science notebook. Leave room to extend the table if necessary.

2. Answer Analysis question 1.

3. Follow your teacher to an outdoor location.

4. Spread your towel and sit down.

5. For 10 minutes, observe the ecosystem quietly. As you do, list the abiotic and biotic factors of this ecosystem on the data table.

6. Pay close attention to one animal in the ecosystem. Watch the animal for a few minutes and try to determine what it is doing. For example, does it seem to be gathering food, traveling, or interacting with another animal? Answer Analysis question 2.

7. After 10 minutes, quietly move to a new spot within the outdoor area.

8. From this new perspective, see if you are aware of any biotic or abiotic factors that you did not see earlier. If so, add them to the data table.

9. Sketch a food web that includes the organisms on the data table.

Analysis

1. What is an ecosystem?

2. What is the source of energy for all ecosystems?

3. Describe the behavior of the animal that you are observing.

4. Is the animal you observed a herbivore, plant eater, or a carnivore, or animal eater? How do you know?

5. How many different types of living things did you observe?

6. A *community* is made up of all of the different populations of living things in an area. Describe the community of this outdoor location.

Data Table	
Abiotic factors	**Biotic factors**

7. You were not able to see the microscopic members of this ecosystem. Where do you think they are located? What are some of the roles of microbes in ecosystems?

8. Describe three of the relationships between abiotic and biotic factors in the ecosystem.

What's Going On?

The ecosystem you observed in this experiment depended on your geographic location. Ecosystems are subunits of *biomes*, large regions that have similar climate and inhabitants. If you live in a prairie ecosystem, the animals you most likely saw today included crows, sparrows, grasshoppers, ground squirrels, and spiders. Crows are glossy, black birds that are described as *omnivores* because they eat both plants and animals. Because crows are not fussy eaters, they are also known as *opportunistic feeders*, animals that will eat whatever is available. By observing crows, you might have seen them walking along the ground picking up grains, fruits, worms, and spiders. They will even scavenge on dead animals and prey on the eggs of other nesting birds.

If you live in a pine or oak forest you may have seen a robin, a gray-brown bird with an orange breast. The birds are omnivores, but they cannot digest hard food. Some of their favorites meals are worms and grubs, the larvae of insects. They also feed on the soft fruits or berries growing on shrubs and small trees. Most often, robins feed on the ground, but prefer to stay close to shrubs or trees where they can fly quickly for cover.

Connections

One of the very few food webs that does not depend on the Sun for energy is found on the floor of the deep ocean. Hot springs, where temperatures reach 716 degrees Fahrenheit (°F) (380 degrees Celsius [°C]), are found at an average depth of 7,300 feet (ft) (2,225 meters [m]), where light never penetrates. The energy to support ecosystems at this depth comes from a chemical source. The hot springs not only supply heat; they also spew out hydrogen sulfide (H_2S), a gas associated with volcanoes. Bacteria that live in the region can chemically change hydrogen sulfide into energy. The bacteria live in *symbiotic relationships* with other organisms, such as clams, mussels, and giant tube worms (Figure 3). In the case of tube worms, the animals lack a mouth or any other components of a digestive system. With billions of bacteria in every ounce of their tissues, they are completely reliant on the microbes for energy. The bacteria are able to use hydrogen sulfide to change carbon dioxide into sugar, which the worms use for food. In return, the worms provide the bacteria with hydrogen sulfide. Their gills, which extend beyond the tube, are filled with *hemoglobin*, a red pigment that binds to hydrogen sulfide and makes it available to the bacteria.

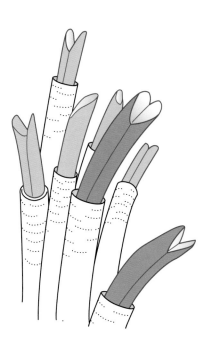

Figure 3

Giant tube worms

Want to Know More?

See appendix for Our Findings.

Further Reading

"Global Ecosystems," September 7, 2009. U.S. Geological Survey. Available online. URL: http://rmgsc.cr.usgs.gov/ecosystems/dataviewer. shtml. Accessed September 14, 2009. On this interactive Web site, one can click on the map to get a description of the ecosystem in that location.

"Major Habitat Types." World Wildlife Federation. Available online. URL: http://www.panda.org/about_our_earth/ecoregions/about/habitat_ types/. Accessed September 12, 2009. The unique characteristics of terrestrial habitats are explained.

Stover, Dawn. "Creatures of the Thermal Vents," Smithsonian Institution. Available online. URL: http://seawifs.gsfc.nasa.gov/OCEAN_PLANET/ HTML/ps_vents.html. Accessed September 14, 2009. Tube worms and sulfur bacteria are important members of a chemosynthetic food web in the deep ocean.

16. Community Succession in Milk

Topic

Succession of a microbial community can be observed in aging milk.

Introduction

A *community* is a group of organisms that live close together and interact with one another. Over time, the environment in which that community exists may be altered through natural changes or the activities of humans. These alterations often cause one species to replace another in dominance within the community. The predictable change in species that make up a community in an ecosystem is called *succession*.

Over time, communities of organisms evolve from simple to complex. Each new species that enters the ecosystem creates changes in the environment. Many ecosystems, but not all, follow an orderly series of changes that begins with a *pioneer species* and concludes with a *climax community*. The pioneer species are the first inhabitants in an area, such as the fast-growing grasses that sprout up in a plowed field or the lichens that appear on rocks following a volcanic eruption. These pioneer organisms change the environment and in doing so create conditions that are less favorable for themselves but more favorable for others. Over time, succession occurs in a series of stages that leads to the final phase, the stable climax community.

Succession can be seen in all types of communities, from bacteria in milk to the plant and animals that live in a forest. In all cases, as the community develops, its environment changes. Some of the classic studies of succession have been done by observing the evolution of a cleared field to an oak and hickory forest (Figure 1). This type of succession takes decades. On the other hand, succession of communities of microorganisms happens much faster. In this experiment, you will observe the succession of microbial communities in milk as it ages.

Time Required

30 minutes for part A
10 minutes a day on 10 follow-up days for part B

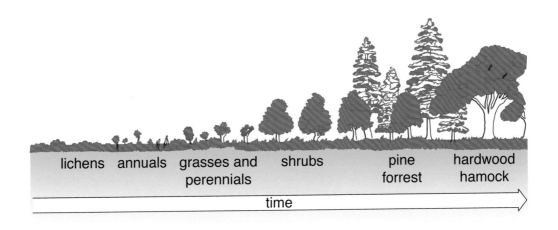

Figure 1

Succession in a cleared field

Materials

- ●◇ glass container with lid (such as a 1-pint mason jar)
- ●◇ incubator
- ●◇ pH paper
- ●◇ pasteurized milk
- ●◇ science notebook

Safety Note Please review and follow the safety guidelines at the beginning of this volume.

Procedure, Part A

1. Fill your glass container about two-thirds full of *pasteurized milk*.
2. Dip a piece of pH paper in the milk. Remove the pH paper and allow it to dry.
3. Compare the color of the paper to the pH chart on the container to find the pH of the milk. In the "starting day" row of the data table, record the pH in the correct column.
4. Look at the milk and note any solids or clumps. Describe the milk under "Consistency" in the starting day row on the data table.

5. Wave your hand over the top of the container toward your nose to carry the odors of the milk through the air. Notice the odor and write your finding under "Odors" in the starting day row on the data table.

6. Loosely fit the lid on top of the container of milk. Place the container in the incubator at 99 degrees Fahrenheit (°F) (37 degrees Celsius [°C]).

Data Table			
	pH	Consistency	Odor
Starting day (day 1)			
Day 2			
Day 3			
Day 4			
Day 5			
Day 6			
Day 7			

Procedure, Part B

1. Each day for the next 6 days, record data on the milk. To do so:
   a. Remove your container of milk from the incubator.
   b. Carefully remove the lid.
   c. Take the pH of the milk.
   d. Observe the milk for changes in consistency and odor.

e. Record your findings on the data table.

f. Loosely place the lid on the container and return the container to the incubator.

2. At the conclusion of the observation period (day 7), dispose of the milk as directed by your teacher.

3. Create a line graph in your science notebook that compares the changes in pH over the seven-day period. Place pH on the Y-axis and time on the X-axis.

Analysis

1. Based on line graph, what happened to the pH of the milk as it aged?

2. Why do you think changes occurred in the pH, consistency, and odor of the milk?

3. Pasteurization does not kill all bacteria in milk: It only destroys deadly bacteria. In the milk sample you tested, what do you think happened to the harmless bacteria that were not destroyed by pasteurization?

4. Not all types of succession are predictable. Do you think the succession of microbes in aging milk is predictable or unpredictable? Defend your answer.

5. During succession new species replace already established species because the environment changes. How did the milk environment change over time?

6. Compare succession in milk to what happens when a plowed field is abandoned.

What's Going On?

Microorganisms are everywhere, and their metabolism and growth vary with the environment in which they are found. If one aspect of an environment changes, all of the organisms found in that environment are affected. Bacteria, like all living things, need nutrients. *Lactose*, the sugar in the milk, is a nutrient for many strains of bacteria.

As the milk aged over the experimental period, the number and species of microorganisms inhabiting the milk changed. On day 1, when the pH was neutral and lactose concentration was high, *lactobacillus* and *streptococcus* flourished (see Figure 2). These two types of bacteria metabolized the lactose, changing it to lactate and *acetic acid*. As a result, the pH of the milk was lowered. The acidic environment caused one of the milk proteins, *casein*, to solidify or *curdle*. In the acidic conditions, the lactobacilli and streptococci died off and were replaced by yeast and bacteria that are acid tolerant. These microorganisms digested the butterfat and gave the milk a putrid smell. This change in microbial communities is an example of succession because modifications in the milk environment enabled new species to flourish.

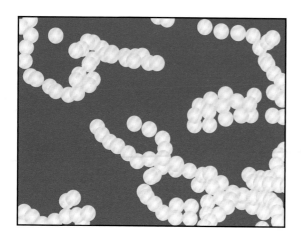 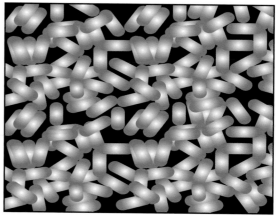

Figure 2

Lactobacillus is a rod-shaped bacterium; streptococcus is round

Connections

Milk contains lactose (a carbohydrate), casein (a protein), and butterfat (a lipid), three nutrients that make excellent media for bacterial growth. Raw milk is dangerous for human consumption because it has not been pasteurized or sterilized. Both harmless and harmful bacteria may be found in raw milk.

Before milk is packaged and delivered to stores, it is heated, a process that destroys the harmful microbes but does not kill all bacteria. The surviving, harmless organisms reproduce as the milk ages, eventually causing the milk to spoil. To slow the bacteria, milk packagers refrigerate the product to reduce the rate of bacterial growth and division. At room temperature or above, bacteria in the milk reproduce quickly.

Want to Know More?

See appendix for Our Findings.

Further Reading

Drape, Joe. "Should This Milk Be Legal?" *New York Times*, August 8, 2007. Available online. URL; http://www.nytimes.com/2007/08/08/dining/08raw.html. Accessed September 12, 2009. Drape discusses the pros and cons of drinking unpasteurized milk.

Pidwirny, Michael. "Plant Succession," May 7, 2009. Available online. URL: http://www.physicalgeography.net/fundamentals/9i.html. Accessed September 12, 2009. Pidwirny explains how the types and number of plants in a community change over time in the process of succession.

University of Guelph. "Dairy Microbiology," Dairy Science and Technology Education Series. Available online. URL: http://www.foodsci.uoguelph.ca/dairyedu/micro.html. Accessed September 12, 2009. This Web site describes the organisms found in the milk environment as it undergoes succession.

Wheatcroft, D. Phil. "Microorganisms in Foods and Around Them," September 30, 2005. Molecular and Cellular Research Team, Agriculture and Agri-Food Canada, Guelph, Ontario. Available online. URL: http://www.magma.ca/~pavel/science/Foodbugs.htm. Accessed September 14, 2009. Wheatcroft discusses the microorganisms found in milk and other agricultural products.

17. Day-Length Adaptations in Seeds

Topic

The rate at which seeds germinate is influenced by the amount of light they receive.

Introduction

A *seed* is an embryonic plant with its food supply wrapped in a protective *seed coat*. Each type of seed is unique, and its particular needs depend on its genetics and the ecological conditions of its habitat. To *germinate*, seeds must have oxygen for the process of *cellular respiration* in which glucose is converted into usable energy. Seeds of all species need energy to carry out their life activities. The exact temperature required for germination varies by species. Some seeds thrive in warm temperatures, while others will germinate under very cool conditions. Water is required by seeds to support the chemical reactions that take place in growing plants. The amount of light a seed needs varies. Some seeds require light before they germinate, but others do not. In this experiment, you will find out if the amount of light affects rate of germination of bean seeds.

Time Required

30 minutes on day 1
25 minutes a day on 5 follow-up days

Materials

- 3 sandwich-size plastic bags
- waterproof marker
- 18 bean seeds
- 6 paper towels

- 3 grow lights or lamps
- access to water
- tape measure
- 2 pieces of graph paper
- science notebook

Safety Note   Please review and follow the safety guidelines at the beginning of this volume.

Procedure, Day 1

1.   Answer Analysis question 1.

2.   Label the plastic bags "4 hours," "8 hours," and "12 hours."

3.   Dampen two paper towels with water. Squeeze out the excess water so that the paper towels are wet but not dripping.

4.   Fold the paper towels and place them in the "4 hours" plastic bag. Position six bean seeds on one side of the paper towels (see Figure 1).

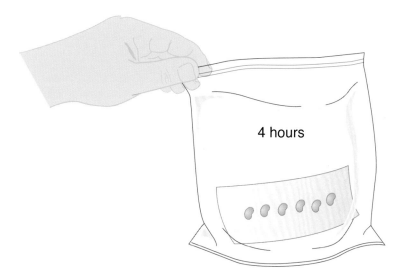

Figure 1

Position seeds on one side of the wet paper towels.

5.   Repeat steps 3 and 4 for the "8 hours" plastic bag.

6. Repeat steps 3 and 4 for the "12 hours" plastic bag.

7. Set up three grow lights or lamps in the same room or in rooms where the temperature is the same. Put a timer on each light. Set the first timer for 4 hours, the second timer for 8 hours, and the third timer for 12 hours.

8. Turn on all three lights. Place the "4-hours" bag of seeds under the 4-hour lamp, seed-side up.

9. Repeat step 8 for the "8 hours" and the "12 hours" bags of seeds.

Procedures, Days 2 through 6

1. Make three copies of the data table. Label one as "4 hours," one as "8 hours," and the last as "12 hours."

2. On day 2, open the "4 hours" bag and examine the seeds. Determine the length of the seedlings (germinating plants). To measure, find the total length of roots and/or shoots extending from the seeds (see Figure 2). Average the lengths of all six seeds and record the length on the 4 hour data table under "Day 2."

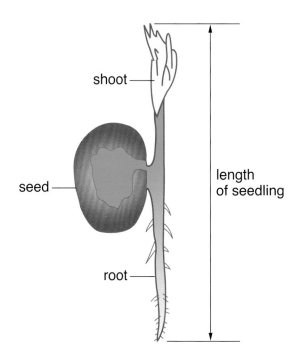

Figure 2

3. Count the number of seeds that have germinated and record the information on the data table.

4. Repeat steps 2 and 3 with the "8 hours" bag of seeds and the "12 hours" bag of seeds.

5. Repeat steps 2 and 3 every day for a total of 5 days. If necessary, remoisten the paper towels.

6. After you have taken measurements on day 6, create a line graph of your findings. Write "Number of days" along the X-axis and "Total number of seeds germinated" on the Y-axis. Show the data from each data table in a different color.

Data Table					
	Day 2	**Day 3**	**Day 4**	**Day 5**	**Day 6**
Average seedling length					
Number of seeds that germinated					

7. Create another line graph with number of days on the X-axis and "Average seedling length" on the Y-axis. Plot your data on this graph.

8. Answer Analysis questions 2 through 5.

Analysis

1. Write a hypothesis on the question, "How does day length affect the rate at which bean seeds germinate?"

2. Examine the data you have recorded on your two graphs. Write a paragraph describing your data and your conclusions. Did your data support your hypothesis?

3. What are some variables in this experiment?

4. Explain how you controlled the variables listed in question 3.

5. Develop an experiment to test the following hypothesis: Seeds require a short exposure to an open flame to germinate.

What's Going On?

Plants in different ecosystems have different *photoperiods*, or reactions to the amount of daylight and dark. In this experiment, you tested one species of plant to see how light affected the rate at which its seeds germinate. The amount of light is the experimental factor, the one you wanted to test. You controlled for several variables, including moisture and temperature.

You placed the seeds on damp paper towels to provide moisture. As the seed coats absorbed moisture, a process known as *imbibition*, they began to swell and split. Water in the seed tissues activated a hormone that set off a series of chemical reactions. The result of these reactions was the conversion of starch stored in the seed into glucose, a simple sugar. The embryonic plant uses glucose to make the energy it needs to start growing. Part of the seed, the *radicle*, grew downward into the soil. Another section, the *plumule*, grew up toward the light (see Figure 3). As the stored starch was used up, newly formed leaves begin to carry out photosynthesis to supply glucose for further growth.

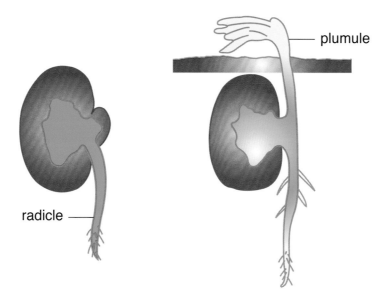

Figure 3

Connections

Many plants require warm temperatures and long hours of sunlight before they will germinate. Some also require a period of cold weather before the warm temperatures. These seeds contain a chemical inhibitor to germination that is gradually worn down at a low temperature. This adaptation prevents plants from germinating during cold seasons when other conditions are not favorable.

The requirements of seeds vary by ecosystem. Seeds of tropical plants are never exposed to varying temperature or periods of sunlight. In the warm, moist environment of the tropics, seeds can safely germinate and grow at any time of year. In many dry ecosystems, seeds remain *dormant* until conditions are favorable. The length of dormancy can vary from a few months to decades. In a few cases, seeds have remained dormant for hundreds of years.

Want to Know More?

See appendix for Our Findings.

Further Reading

Keeley, Jon, E., and C. J. Foteringham. "Smoke-induced Seed Germination in California Chaparral," October 1998. *Ecology*. Available online. URL: http://findarticles.com/p/articles/mi_m2120/is_n7_v79/ ai_21231379/. Accessed September 15, 2009. The authors explain how some seeds need a fire to germinate and remain dormant until heat or chemicals of combustion trigger their germination.

"Process That Regulates Seed Germination Identified," March 18, 2009. *ScienceDaily*. Available online. URL: http://www.sciencedaily. com/releases/2009/03/090311170637.htm. Accessed September 15, 2009. Scientists have recently identified a gene that influences the release of hormones that trigger germination.

Scopel, A., C. L. Ballaré, and R. A. Sánchez. "Awakened by a Flash of Sunlight," August 2002. *Plant Physiology*. Available online. URL: http://4e. plantphys.net/article.php?ch=&id=235. Accessed September 20, 2009. Scopel, Ballaré, and Sánchez explain how sunlight triggers responses in seeds.

18. How Effective Is Mimicry?

Topic

Some species are able to avoid predators by mimicking the appearance of poisonous species.

Introduction

Predators are always on the lookout for their next meal. To protect themselves, prey have developed *adaptations* that help them avoid being eaten. Some species of prey animals have evolved toxins that deter their predators. For example, the larvae of monarch butterflies (see Figure 1) graze on the toxic sap of milkweed. The bodies of these insects retain the toxin when they develop into adults. If a bird consumes the monarch butterfly, it gets sick and vomits. Birds quickly learn to avoid this nauseating prey.

monarch butterfly   viceroy butterfly

Figure 1

The monarch butterfly on the left has several mimics, including the viceroy on the right.

To warn predators of their poisonous nature, prey display bright *aposematic* or warning coloration. When a predator feeds on its first aposematic prey, the individual prey animal usually dies. However, the predator learns a lesson and other individuals of the species benefit. Species that resemble the poisonous prey benefit because predators also avoid them. Some species of snakes use this system. Coral snakes (Figure 2), which are venomous, have bright colors that warn predators to stay away. These relatively small snakes have evolved vivid warning colors of red, white, and black that are displayed in bands. Similar colors and bands are found on harmless corn snakes and king snakes. In this experiment, you will determine whether mimicry helps a prey animal survive.

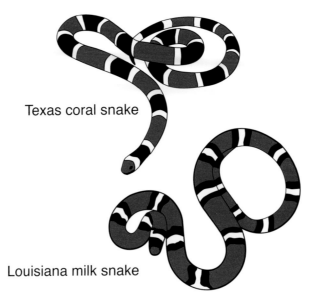

Texas coral snake

Louisiana milk snake

Figure 2

The Louisiana milk snake (below) resembles the Texas coral snake (above).

Time Required

45 minutes

Materials

- 100 dried pinto beans
- beaker or paper cup to hold the pinto beans
- waterproof red marker
- pencil
- stopwatch
- science notebook

Procedure

1. Work in groups of four. Three people will play the roles of predators. Designate these individuals as "predator 1," "predator 2," and "predator 3." The fourth person will serve as the timekeeper.

2. The pinto beans will be the prey. Draw a bold, red X on each side of 25 pinto beans. These represent prey that are poisonous.

3. Draw a bold, red straight line on each side of another 25 pinto beans. These represent prey that resemble the poisonous species, but are not toxic.

4. Put all 100 pinto beans into the beaker or paper cup. Stir the beans gently with a pencil to mix. Carefully pour the beans onto your desktop.

5. When the timekeeper says "Go," predator 1 picks up pinto beans for 2 seconds. The predator can only pick up one bean at a time. If the predator fails to pick up five beans, it "dies" and is taken out of play. If the predator picks up a bean with an X, it dies and is taken out of play. After the first round of feeding, predator 1 records the number of unmarked pintos, pintos with Xs, and pintos with straight lines on the data table under Round 1. Return all the beans to the cup.

6. Repeat step 5 for predators 2 and 3. Continue in the manner for a total of five rounds fo each predator.

7. Find the average number of unmarked pintos, pintos with Xs, and pintos with straight lines collected by each predator.

Analysis

1. In your own words, define *mimicry*.
2. Are mimics usually poisonous or nonpoisonous? Explain.
3. In this activity, why did the predators avoid the pinto beans with red Xs?
4. Examine the data table. Which type of bean was most often picked up: unmarked pinto beans or pinto beans with red lines?
5. Based on this experiment, what conclusions can you draw about the effectiveness of mimicry as a defense mechanism?

Data Table						
	Round 1	**Round 2**	**Round 3**	**Round 4**	**Round 5**	**Average**
Predator 1						
Unmarked						
Xs						
Straight lines						
Predator 2						
Unmarked						
Xs						
Straight lines						
Predator 3						
Unmarked						
Xs						
Straight lines						

What's Going On?

To avoid pinto beans with red *X*s, which represent warning coloration on toxic prey, the predators in this experiment picked up unmarked pinto beans first. These unmarked beans were easy to identify as safe to eat. Prey found that trying to differentiate between beans with *X*s and beans with a similar coloration—straight red lines—took more time. As a result, at the end of the experiment, predators had collected few if any of the pinto beans with straight red lines. The presence of these lines made them resemble the "toxic" prey and thus protected them from the predators.

The type of predator protection described in this experiment is *Batesian mimicry*, named after the English naturalist Henry Walter Bates (1825–92). The toxic organism is the *model* while the organism imitating the model it the *mimic*. Although this strategy helps protect the mimic, is puts the model at a disadvantage. If predators dine on the mimics first, they do not learn the lesson and consequently do not associate the warning coloration with danger.

Connections

Batesian mimicry is not the only way that animals protect themselves from predators. In *self-mimicry* animals display large eyespots (Figure 3) on some body part that is not close to the head. A predator usually attacks its prey near the head to ensure a kill. Attacks to regions along the outer part of the body are easier for the prey to survive.

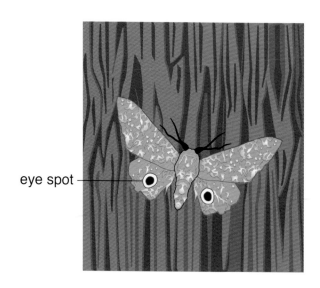

eye spot

Figure 3

This moth displays a false eye spot to confuse its predators.

Another protective technique is *cryptic coloration*, patterns, colors, and shapes that hide the prey from its predators. For example, the stripes of a zebra help it blend in with tall grasses, making it more difficult for predators to locate. One form of cryptic coloration is *camouflage*, a technique in which prey animals look like the environment. A mantis is an insect that looks so much like a twig that predators often overlook it.

Some animals, like clams, turtles, or armadillos, are protected by armor. Porcupines have sharp quills that protect them. Still other species stay alive by avoiding prey. Running, swimming, or flying away can protect a prey animal. To warn other members of the prey species, animals may release alarm *pheromones*, chemical signals, or give high-pitched alarm calls. Other animals produce offensive odors to repel predators. The skunk is the best known species for using this chemical defense.

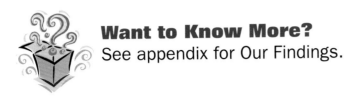

Want to Know More?
See appendix for Our Findings.

Further Reading

Goodman, Susan E. "On the Menu," *National Geographic*, March 2005. Available online. URL: http://magma.nationalgeographic.com/ngexplorer/0503/articles/mainarticle.html. Accessed September 21, 2009. Goodman discusses several adaptations that help prey avoid their predators.

Mallet, James, and Kevin Fowler. Warning Colour and Mimicry, "Evolutionary Genetics," 2007. Department of Genetics, Evolution and Environment, University College London. Available online. URL: http://www.ucl.ac.uk/~ucbhdjm/courses/b242/Mimic/Mimic.html. Accessed September 21, 2009. The authors explain the adaptive advantages of warning coloration.

Williamson, David. "Study of Poisonous Snakes Boosts Old Batesian Principle of Mimicry," March 15, 2001. University of North Carolina New Service, *EurekAlert*. Available online. URL: http://www.anapsid.org/batesianmimicry.html. Accessed September 21, 2009. Williamson's experiments with model king snakes and coral snakes support the theory put forth by Henry Bates in 1862.

19. Identifying the Benthos Community

Topic

A variety of animals can be found living in the benthos of a pond or lake.

Introduction

If you have ever waded into a pond or lake, you may have felt soft mud or sand between your toes. The layer of soil and rocks at the bottom of a body of water is the *benthos*. Many different types of *macroinvertebrates*, small animals without backbones that are visible to the naked eye, make their homes here (see Figure 1). Most abundant are the wormlike larvae of aquatic insects such as mayflies, caddis flies, and stone flies. Another common animal is the aquatic *annelid* worm, segmented like its terrestrial cousin but smaller. Also present are clams and snails, two types of mollusks. Some locations house bug-like amphipods, aquatic sow bugs (Figure 1f), and crayfish. In this experiment, you will collect and identify the benthic organisms in a freshwater body of water.

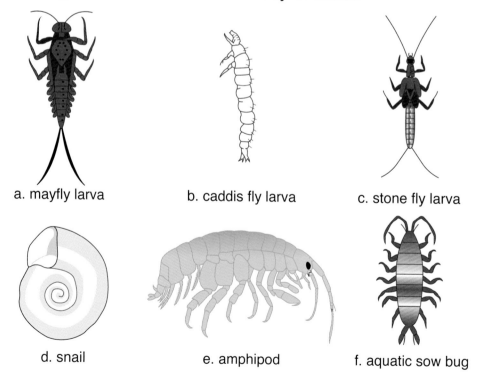

a. mayfly larva b. caddis fly larva c. stone fly larva

d. snail e. amphipod f. aquatic sow bug

Figure 1

Time Required

55 minutes for Part A
45 minutes for Part B

Materials

- ●◇ dip net
- ●◇ grab sampler
- ●◇ small shovel
- ●◇ sieve with U.S. standard #60 or #30 mesh screen
- ●◇ yardstick
- ●◇ tweezers or forceps
- ●◇ white enamel or plastic tray (big enough to hold the material collected by a grab sample)
- ●◇ small collection jars with lids
- ●◇ small bottle of formalin
- ●◇ 2 Petri dishes
- ●◇ access to the Internet or books on benthic organisms
- ●◇ hand lens or dissecting microscope
- ●◇ science notebook

> **Safety Note**   Wear old sneakers or waders and clothing that can get wet. Stay with the instructor when working outdoors near a body of water. Wear gloves and goggles when working with formalin. Please review and follow the safety guidelines at the beginning of this volume.

Procedure, Part A

1. Follow your teacher outdoors to a freshwater body of water such as a pond, lake, or stream.
2. Examine the benthos at the water's edge. In your science notebook, describe the *substrate*, the material making up the benthos, as soft (muddy), gravely, sandy, or hard (rocky).

3. At a depth of about 1 foot (ft) (0.305 meters [m]) of water, use a dip net to sweep across the substrate. Move the net back and forth several times to collect any organisms living on top of the substrate.

4. Empty the organisms into the white pan.

5. Use tweezers to separate organisms in the pan from sand, stones, twigs, and other nonliving materials that you may have also harvested in the dip net. Transfer the organisms to a collection jar. Add enough formalin to the jar to cover the organisms. Label the jar "above substrate sample, site 1."

6. Use the grab sampler to collect some soil at the same location.

7. Empty the contents of the grab sampler into a white pan.

8. Use the small shovel to transfer some of the grab sampler material onto the sieve. While holding the sieve in the water, gently shake the apparatus from side to side, washing the material with water. Repeat until all of the material in the grab sample has been sieved. Transfer the contents of the sieve to a collection jar. Add enough formalin to the jar to cover the organisms. Label the jar "substrate grab sample, site 1."

9. Repeat steps 2 through 8 at another site in the shallow water.

Procedure, Part B

1. In the classroom, rinse the samples in the collection jars in water to remove the formalin.

2. To sort through the samples, place some of the material in half of a Petri dish and examine it with a hand lens or under the dissecting microscope. Use forceps or tweezers to separate organisms from nonliving material. Transfer organisms to a clean half of a Petri dish.

3. Use taxonomic references and the pictures in Figure 1 to help identify the organisms. Record the names and the numbers of organisms you collected in your science notebook.

Analysis

1. What were the most common types of organisms you collected with the dip net?

2. What were the most common types of organisms you collected with the grab sampler?

3. Calculate the relative abundance of the most abundant organisms you collected. To do so, divide the number of organisms by the total number of macroinvertebrates you collected.

4. Some benthic invertebrates eat algae and bacteria. These invertebrates are then eaten by fish. How might the loss of these invertebrates affect the ecosystem?

5. Suppose you went back to the same site and sampled macroinvertebrates again six months from now and found that only two of the species you saw today are still living there. Suggest some reasons for this type of drastic change in the benthos community.

What's Going On?

Organisms that make up the benthic community are highly diverse. The specific invertebrates found in benthic samples vary, depending on the characteristics of the ecosystem. These organisms make up an important part of the freshwater food chain. They feed on algae and bacteria and in turn serve as food for fish.

To the novice, distinguishing the larvae of insects can be difficult. These wormlike animals hatch from eggs that are laid in the water by adult insects. Immature stone flies and mayflies especially resemble each other. To distinguish between the two, first observe the claws on each leg. Stone flies have two claws on each leg and mayflies have one. Next count the number of filaments in the tail. Two filaments represent mayflies; stone flies have three.

Caddis fly larvae are easily distinguished because these animals build protective cases around their bodies. Each species constructs a unique case from soil particles, twigs, and debris held together by silky threads produced in their mouths. Caddis fly larvae lack the filamentous tails found on stone flies and mayflies. Instead they have small leg-like structures on their abdomens.

Connections

Benthic organisms are important in *biomonitoring*, the use of living things to gauge the health of an ecosystem. If a body of freshwater is exposed to pollutants, the chemicals settle into the sediment and affect the number and health of animals living there. Macroinvertebrates are especially useful in biomonitoring because they are found in almost all freshwater systems. In addition, the animals are *sedentary*, so they do not swim or crawl to a new location if their homes become polluted.

In biomonitoring, scientists identify several *indicator species*, organisms whose health is indicative of pollutant levels. These are usually the organisms that are most sensitive to changes in the environment. Although benthic macroinvertebrates are commonly used, fish and certain species of algae can also fill this role. Scientists who rely on macroinvertebrates check on changes in their appearance, biochemistry, and physiology and relate these changes to particular changes or pollutants in the environment.

One common problem found in freshwater communities is low oxygen levels. Some pollutants cause *algal blooms*, overgrowth of algae. When the algae die, they fall to the sediment where they are broken down by oxygen-consuming bacteria. Large numbers of these bacteria can use up all of the available oxygen, causing the death of most benthic organisms.

One group of organisms that can tolerate low oxygen is the segmented worms (see Figure 2). These animals are delicate and small, usually less than one inch (in.) (2.5 centimeters [cm]) long. Special adaptations make it possible for the worms to survive in a low oxygen environment. A segmented worm has a thin body wall which enables oxygen to diffuse into the blood. In addition, the blood of these aquatic worms contains a pigment that helps bind oxygen.

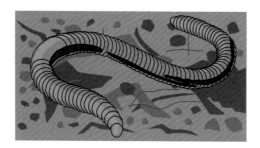

Figure 2

Segmented worm

Want to Know More?

See appendix for Our Findings.

Further Reading

"About Biological Indicators," June 18, 2009. U.S. Environmental Protection Agency. Available online. URL: http://www.epa.gov/bioindicators/html/about.html. Accessed September 22, 2009. This site discusses the value of biological indicators and provides links to several related Web pages.

"Aquatic Macroinvertebrate Identification Key," March 1, 1999. Available online. URL: http://people.virginia.edu/~sos-iwla/Stream-Study/Key/MacroKeyIntro.HTML. Accessed September 24, 2009. This Web site provides a taxonomic key for identifying stream macroinvertebrates.

"Common Stream Invertebrates," 2008. New Hampshire Department of Environmental Services. Available online. URL: http://des.nh.gov/organization/divisions/water/wmb/biomonitoring/edinv.htm. Accessed September 22, 2009. This Web site provides great descriptions of several types of macroinvertebrates.

Feminella, Jack W., and Kathryn M. Flynn. "The Alabama Watershed Demonstration Project: Biotic Indicators of Water Quality," Alabama A & M and Auburn Universities, December, 1999. Available online. URL: http://www.aces.edu/pubs/docs/A/ANR-1167/ANR-1167.pdf. Accessed September 22, 2009. This Web site provides excellent photographs of some invertebrates used in biomonitoring.

Hoosier Riverwatch. "Taxonomic Key to Stream Macroinvertebrates," Indiana Department of Natural Resources. Available online. URL: http://www.in.gov/dnr/nrec/files/HR05_Chapter5_3.pdf. Accessed September 23, 2009. This is an excellent key developed for novices who are monitoring macroinvertebrates in stream studies.

20. Water Affects Temperatures in Biomes

Topic
Rainfall impacts how quickly the temperature of a biome drops after the Sun goes down.

Introduction

Biomes, major biological communities over large areas of land, have unique climates and life-forms. All living things in a biome are affected by the interaction of both living and nonliving factors. *Abiotic*, or nonliving, factors include light, rainfall, temperature, cloud cover, oxygen availability, and soil type. Some of the *biotic*, or living, factors include reproductive rate of a species and each organism's position in the food chain. The ecology of a biome is the sum total of interactions that occur between the biotic and abiotic factors.

Of the terrestrial biomes on Earth, the tropical rain forest (Figure 1) and the desert (Figure 2) represent the extremes. The amount of rainfall in each biome has a direct impact on life-forms found there and well as abiotic factors such as humidity and temperature. The desert biome, which gets less than 10 inches (in.) (25.4 centimeters [cm]) of rain a year, cools rapidly when the Sun sets, and heats quickly when the Sun rises. During the day, the desert may reach more than 100 degrees Fahrenheit (°F) (38 degrees Celsius [°C]), but at night its temperatures can dip to between 40°F and 50°F (4°C to 10°C). Because the desert soil is dry, little water evaporates into the air, keeping the *relative humidity* low, ranging from 10 to 20 percent.

The tropical rain forest, the wettest biome on Earth, receives from 79 to 177 in. (200 to 450 cm) of rain each year. The humidity is extremely high and temperatures are relatively constant, fluctuating only within in a very narrow range. Daytime temperatures vary from 86°F to 95°F (30°C to 35°C). When the Sun goes down, the temperatures range from around 68°F to 77°F (20°C to 25°C).

Organisms living in these two vastly different biomes have *adaptations*, specialized traits, that enable them to survive in their habitats. Desert animals have special adaptations for treacherous droughts and extremes in temperature. On the other hand, organisms in the tropical rain forests deal with wet conditions and relatively stable temperatures. In this experiment, you will explore how the amount of moisture affects the nighttime temperatures of a biome.

Figure 1

The tropical rain forest is extremely humid.

Figure 2

Deserts are very dry biomes.

Time Required

55 minutes

Materials

- 2 test tubes
- large beaker
- 2 Celsius thermometers, each fitted in a 1-hole rubber stopper
- sand (about 1/4 cup)
- water (about 1/4 cup)
- test-tube rack
- test-tube holder
- clock with a second hand
- hot plate
- 2 different color pens
- science notebook

| **Safety Note** | Take care when working with the hot plate and beakers of hot water. Please review and follow the safety guidelines at the beginning of this volume. |

Procedure

1. Fill a large beaker about half full of water.
2. Place the beaker on a hot plate. Adjust the hot plate to the high setting.
3. Fill a test tube one-half full of water and another test tube one-half full of sand.
4. Place the rubber stopper and thermometer assemblies into the test tubes so the thermometer bulbs are submerged beneath the sand in one test tube and the water in the other. Make sure the bulbs reach equal depths in both the water and the sand (see Figure 3).

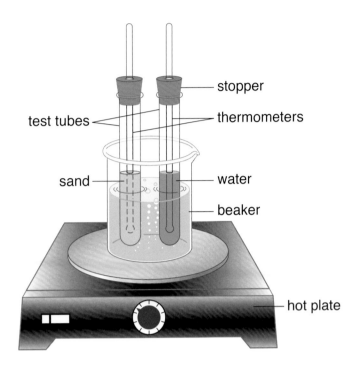

Figure 3

5. Use the test-tube holder to position gently each test tube in the beaker of water that is heating on the hot plate.

6. Allow the tests tubes to heat until one of the test tubes reaches 158°F (70°C). When this occurs, use the test-tube holder to remove that test-tube from the beaker of hot water. Place this test tube in the test-tube rack, and begin your measurements (step 7). Do not remove the other test-tube until it has reached the 158°F (70°C) mark and then begin its measurements.

7. Once a test tube has been removed from the beaker of hot water, record its temperature on the data table every 2 minutes for a total of 20 minutes.

	Data Table										
	Starting temp.	2 min	4 min	6 min	8 min	10 min	12 min	14 min	16 min	18 min	20 min
Test of water	158°F										
Test tube with sand	158°F										

8. Use the data on the data table to create a line graph in your science notebook that compares the decline in temperature in each test tube over 20 minutes. To do so:

    a. Place temperature on the Y-axis and time on the X-axis.

    b. Plot the data for both test tubes on the same graph.

    c. Use two different color pens to represent the data from the two test tubes.

Analysis

1. Based on the line graphs, did the test tube of sand or the test tube of water lose the most heat over the 20-minute period?

2. Which test tube represented the desert biome and which one represented the tropical rain forest? Explain your answer.

3. Do you think areas of land close to large bodies of water cool more quickly or more slowly at night than areas of land not surrounded by water? Defend your answer.

4. What other abiotic factors do you think influence life in the desert and tropical rain forest?

5. What do you think might happen if you moved some of the desert animals to the tropical rain forest and vice versa? Would the difference in abiotic factors impact their survival?

6. If you had measured the temperature decline in a test tube of gravel over 20 minutes, how do you think the results would compare to those for the sand and water? Explain your reasoning.

What's Going On?

Sunlight striking the Earth heats up the surface. Some materials warm gradually and hold heat for a long time. Other materials warm quickly and just as rapidly give off heat energy. The ability of a material to take up and store heat is referred to as its *specific heat capacity*.

Water is a vast heat reservoir because it has a high specific heat capacity. Water holds heat better than dry sand or soil and gives off heat energy to the air slowly. As a result, air over water stays warm longer than air over land. Because the desert lacks moisture, it warms quickly in the day and cools rapidly at night. The extremely hot daytime temperatures and cool nights explain why many of the desert's inhabitants are *nocturnal*, active only at night. During the day, the animals sleep in cool dens, caves or burrows.

Because of daily rains, the soil in a tropical rain forest is saturated by water, and some of this water evaporates into the air, creating very humid conditions. As a result, this biome warms gradually when the Sun comes up and releases the heat slowly at night. Animals of the tropical rain forest do not have to restrict their activities to the night hours.

Connections

Water's ability to act as a heat reservoir is due to its chemical structure. Water molecules are *polar*; one end has a slight positive charge and the other end a slight negative charge. These oppositely charged ends attract each other, forming *hydrogen bonds* (see Figure 4).

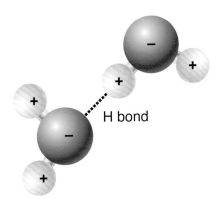

Figure 4

Polar water molecules form hydrogen bonds.

Heat is a measure of molecular motion. When water is heated, energy is first used to break the hydrogen bonds. Once the bonds are broken, the water molecules begin to vibrate and the temperature goes up. The reverse is also true. When water cools, hydrogen bonds begin to form between molecules. Once the bonds are established, the water molecules slow their movements and the temperature begins to drop.

 Want to Know More?

See appendix for Our Findings.

Further Reading

"Specific Heat Capacities of Some Common Substances,"
2005. Engineering Toolbox. Available online. URL: http://www.
engineeringtoolbox.com/specific-heat-capacity-d_391.html. Accessed
September 23, 2009. This Web site provides the specific heat capacities
of water, soil, muddy soil, and other materials.

Sydenham, S., and R. Thomas. "Desert Biome," 2002. Available online.
URL: http://www.kidcyber.com.au/topics/biomedes2.htm. Accessed
September 23, 2009. This Planet Earth Web page describes plants and
animals in desert biomes.

Wheeling Jesuit University. "Biomes," April 28, 2005. Available online.
URL: http://www.cotf.edu/ete/modules/msese/earthsysflr/biomes.html.
Accessed September 23, 2009. The easy-to-understand explanation of
biomes includes links to related topics.

Scope and Sequence Chart

This chart aligns the experiments in this book with some of the National Science Content Standards. (These experiments do not address every national science standard.) Please refer to your local and state content standards for additional information. As always, adult supervision is recommended and discretion should be used in selecting experiments appropriate to each age group or to individual students.

Standard	Grades 5–8	Grades 9–12
Physical Science		
Properties and changes of properties in matter		
Chemical reactions		
Motions and forces		
Transfer of energy and interactions of energy and matter	20	20
Conservation of energy and increase in disorder		
Life Science		
Cells and structure and function in living systems		
Reproduction and heredity		
Regulation and behavior	8	8

Standard	Grades 5–8	Grades 9–12
Populations and ecosystems	1, 2, 3, 4, 5, 6, 7, 12, 13, 14, 15, 19	1, 2, 3, 4, 5, 6, 7, 12, 13, 14, 15, 19
Diversity and adaptations of organisms	2, 8, 17, 18	2, 8, 17, 18
Interdependence of organisms	7, 10, 11, 16, 20	7, 10, 11, 16, 20
Matter, energy, and organization in living systems	4, 6, 9, 12, 13	4, 6, 9, 12, 13
Biological evolution	18	18
Earth Science		
Structure and energy in the Earth system	12, 20	12, 20
Geochemical cycles	13	13
Origin and evolution of the Earth system		
Origin and evolution of the universe		
Earth in the solar system		
Nature of Science		
Science in history		
Science as an endeavor	all	all

Grade Level

Setting

The experiments are classified by materials and equipment use as follows:

- Those under SCHOOL LABORATORY involve materials and equipment found only in science laboratories. Those under SCHOOL LABORATORY must be carried out there under the supervision of the teacher or another adult.

- Those under HOME involve household or everyday materials. Some of these can be done at home, but call for supervision.

- The experiments classified under OUTDOORS may be done at the school or at the home, but call for supervision.

SCHOOL LABORATORY

8.   Surface Area Affects Body Temperature

20.   Water Affects Temperatures in Biomes

HOME

1.   Size or Age Distributions in Populations

6.   Food Webs

7.   Biome Learning Centers

9.   Predator and Prey Populations

11.   Observing Plant Growth in Different Biomes

13.   The Role of Decomposers in the Nitrogen Cycle

14.   Invasive Species' Impact on an Ecosystem

16.   Community Succession in Milk

17.   Day-Length Adaptations in Seeds

18.   How Effective Is Mimicry?

OUTDOORS

Our Findings

1. SIZE OR AGE DISTRIBUTIONS IN POPULATIONS

Idea for class discussion: Show students a crosscut of a tree trunk (or a picture of a crosscut). Discuss the fact that each ring represents a year of growth. Show the students that some rings are very close together while others are farther apart. Elicit from the class the meaning of these differences.

Analysis

1. The graph shows that most of the oaks are young trees while most of the pines are middle aged trees so oaks is the younger population.

2. The oaks population is faster growing because it has more young individuals.

3. Answers will vary. Students might say that only trees that have been cut can be analyzed using this method.

4. Answers will vary based on student findings.

5. Answers will vary. The diameter of a tree does not necessarily reflect its age. Some trees growing in shade could have stunted growth because they do not have as many resources as larger, canopy trees.

6. a. A; There are no young trees on the golf course, indicating that they have been cut down; b. Data Table 3; c. Data Table 2

2. SPECIES DIVERSITY

Idea for class discussion: Ask students to list the organism that they would expect to find in the area where you will be collecting data today. After the experiment, contrast their expectations to their findings.

Notes to the teacher: Before class, select an outdoor area where students can collect data. Any outdoor area will work, whether a park, a lawn, or a forest. You may want to mark off an area with tape or have students measure a quadrant in which they will count species. If the area is large, all students can work within it; or give each group of students a relatively small area in which to work.

Analysis

1. Answers will vary. Biodiversity is the variety of life-forms in an area.
2. Figure 2, community B
3. 0.025
4. 0.40
5. Answers will vary depending on the area students analyzed.
6. Answers will vary. Farming reduces biodiversity because it kills unwanted plants to make room for a few desired species.

3. MONITORING VEGETATIVE COVER

Idea for class discussion: To find out how aware students are of ground cover, ask them to describe the ground cover in three regions near the school or regions they have visited. Discuss reasons for differences in ground cover in different locations. Determine which areas have natural ground cover and which have cover that was planted.

Analysis

1. Ecologists can learn the predominant plants in the ecosystem and understand the availability of water.
2. Answers will vary.
3. Answers will vary.
4. Answers will vary.
5. a. 9; b. 5; c. 55.6 percent

4. LEAF AREA AFFECTS PRIMARY PRODUCTIVITY

Idea for class discussion: Ask pairs of students to discuss the possible meaning of the term *primary productivity* as it relates to an ecosystem. Have one or two pairs share their thoughts with the class.

Analysis

1. NPP takes into account the use of glucose (and therefore carbon dioxide) to sustain plant life; GPP does not.
2. Cellular respiration uses energy. Photosynthesis stores energy.
3. Answers will vary. One advantage is accuracy of measurement. A disadvantage is that the plant is stripped of all its leaves.

4. A drought, or any other condition that damages leaves or causes a loss of leaves, reduces a plant's productivity.

5. Answers will vary depending plants measured.

6. Answers will vary. Students might cut a leaf into geometric shapes, find the area of each shape, then add the shapes to find the total area. Or they might trace the leaf on graph paper, count the number of boxes within the tracing, and find the area.

5. DIVERSITY IN SOIL ECOSYSTEMS

Idea for class discussion: Ask students to list some specific organisms that they might find in the soil. Discuss the requirements for life that the soil environment must provide for all of these organisms: food, water, oxygen (for the macro organisms), and space. Help students understand how those requirements are met in the soil.

Notes to the teacher: Select three distinctly different soil sites. Make sure that one site is a high traffic area with compacted soil and that another site sees little traffic and has loose soil. Demonstrate the use of the berlese funnel and invertebrate pit trap. Show students that they can put a soil sample in a dishpan and add water to separate soil from invertebrates in the soil. As students are writing their experiments, remind them that they are comparing the number of different kinds of invertebrates at the three sites. They do not have to be able to identify the invertebrates.

Analysis

1. Soil invertebrates need space, food, water, and oxygen.

2. Answers will vary based on students' observations.

3. Answers will vary but might include the use of a pitfall trap.

4. Answers will vary based on experimental results.

5. Answers will vary but might include worms, millipedes, or spiders.

6. Answers will vary based on experimental results.

6. FOOD WEBS

Idea for class discussion: Ask pairs of students to discuss what they eat in a typical day. Determine how much of their food is plant material and how much is animal material.

Notes to the teacher: Some examples of food chains include:

grass leaves → grasshopper → toad → garter snake

weed seeds → gopher → weasel

grass seeds → ground squirrel → hawk

weed stems → caterpillar → spider → sparrow

grass stems → vole → coyote

Analysis

1. plants

2. producer to consumer

3. phytoplankton → zooplankton → small fish → large fish → seals → whales

4. six

5. Answers will vary but could include fungi and bacteria.

6. Without decomposers dead plants and animals would not break down and the nutrients tied up in their bodies would not be released.

7. Producers convert the Sun's energy into chemical energy that organisms can use to maintain life.

8. Answers will vary. Scavengers eat dead and decaying organisms.

9. a. grass and weed parts; b. grasshopper, gopher, ground squirrel, caterpillar, vole; c. Answers will vary but could include toad, weasel, hawk spider, coyote; d. Answers will vary but may include snake, hawk, or coyote.

7. BIOME LEARNING CENTERS

Idea for class discussion: Ask students to list the biomes of the world on the board. Find out if students can identify their own biome.

Analysis

1. 60 to 90 days

2. The arctic is found only in North America while the alpine tundra is found in mountainous regions. Weather may not be as cold as Arctic tundra as in the alpine tundra.

3. desert

4. Beneath the upper layer of the soil is a year-round region of ice, the permafrost.

5. Animals have thick fur that traps air and acts as insulation. Many also have a lot of body fat that helps keep them warm. Some animals hibernate for the winter while others travel south.

6. birches, willows, lichens, mosses, and grasses

7. Many taiga trees have needlelike leaves. (These do not hold snow and ice, reducing the number of tree limbs broken by heavy precipitation. In addition, they have a small surface area, preventing the loss of moisture from the plant.)

8. 6 months

9. taiga

10. temperate deciduous forest

11. temperate rain forest

12. Loss of leaves enables the trees to be dormant during the winter.

13. the tilt of the Earth on its axis

14. Cold deserts receive more rainfall than hot ones.

15. Chihuahuan, Great Basin, Mojave, and Sonoran

16. Sahara

17. Answers will vary. Many stay underground during the day. Most have organs that conserve water.

18. Deserts are very dry, and dry air does not hold heat as well as moist air. When the Sun goes down, the desert heat radiates into space.

19. Tropic of Cancer and Tropic of Capricorn

20. in the Pacific Northwest

21. The tropical rain forest is warmer and has more species of trees. The trees are younger than those in a temperate rain forest.

22. tall grass prairie, mixed grass prairie, short grass prairie

23. bison and pronghorns

24. Antarctica

8. SURFACE AREA AFFECTS BODY TEMPERATURE

Idea for class discussion: Pose this question: Which animal cools the fastest, a large one or a small one? Let students explain their reasoning.

Analysis

1. Answers will vary based on students' procedures.

2. a. 250 ml beaker; b. 150 ml beaker; c. 50 ml beaker

3. Answers will vary based on experimental results.

4. The greater an animal's body size, the more slowly it loses heat.

5. from food

6. A small one because small animals lose a lot of heat and must replace the lost energy by eating.

7. Answers will vary but could include amount of light, pH of the water, types of beakers, and starting temperature of the water.

9. PREDATOR AND PREY POPULATIONS

Idea for class discussion: Ask students to identify some predators and their prey. Ask the question: What would happen to the size of a predator population if all of the prey disappeared?

Analysis

1. a. about 55,000; b. about 15,000; c. about 5,000; d. about 90,000; e. small

2. No. Sometimes the lynx landed on the desktop without touching a hare.

3. As the predator population increased in size, the prey population decreased.

4. Answers will vary. As the number of predators increase, the prey decrease. As a result the predators decrease. This leads to an increase in the number of prey.

10. WHAT ARE THE STAGES OF ECOLOGICAL SUCCESSION?

Idea for class discussion: Ask students to define the term *ecological succession*. Have the modify their definitions after the experiment.

Notes to the teacher: Select several areas on campus or near the school where students can see sign of succession such as weeds growing in a flower bed or plants pushing their way through pavement. If you cannot take students outdoors, show them photographs or slides.

Analysis

1. Answers will vary. *Succession* is the changes that a community undergoes over time.

2. Primary succession takes place in a region that has never been colonized. Secondary succession occurs in a place that has supported life.

3. ___P__ A volcanic eruption forms a new island in the Pacific Ocean.

   ___S__ Fire destroys a forest.

   ___S__ A central city park is abandoned.

   ___P__ After a hurricane, sand dunes are created behind existing dunes.

   ___S__A paved street is rarely used.

4. Answers will vary. Students might explain that humans remove natural vegetation and alter the normal development of climax communities.

5. Some animals feed on plants and cannot move into an area before food is available.

6. a. Rocks and a few pioneer species are present. b. Soil is beginning to develop, and more plants are present. c. Small shrubs have moved in. d. Large trees have moved in.

7. a. grasses; b. large trees; c. stages a, b, and c; d. Large trees reduce the amount of light that reaches the soil.

8. top row: left, 4; Right, 1; bottom row: left, 3; right, 2

11. OBSERVING PLANT GROWTH IN DIFFERENT BIOMES

Idea for class discussion: Ask students to describe the local climate in terms of temperature and precipitation. Have them list some of the characteristic plants and animals in the immediate area. Point out that the climate and the organisms that live there are characteristic of a biome.

Notes to the teacher: Earth's major terrestrial biomes are desert, tundra, taiga, temperate deciduous forest, grassland, savanna, temperate rain forest, temperate seasonal forest, and tropical rain forest. Assign two biomes to each laboratory group (omitting the cold ones unless you have plenty of refrigerator and freezer space).

Analysis

1. Answers will vary. A biome is a large geographic region with uniform climate, plants, and animals.

2. Answers will vary. Student could have used a lamp or grow light with a timer, or they could have moved the pots into and out of the light from windows.

3. Answers will vary based on students' experimental results.

4. Answers will vary, but probably not.

5. Answers will vary based on students' experimental results.

6. Answers will vary, but probably not.

7. Answers will vary. The tundra and taiga are very cold climates. The tundra supports only a few types of cold hearty plants.

8. Plants have adaptations for the biomes in which they live. By raising the same three plants in all biomes, one can see that some conditions yielded higher productivity than others.

12. ENERGY IN ECOSYSTEMS

Idea for class discussion: Ask students to describe some of the plants that grow near the school. As a class, create a list of ideas about how these plants impact the ecosystem in which the school is located.

Analysis

1. Some of the energy from the Sun is reflected back into space.

2. Answers will vary.

3. Answers will vary. Abiotic factors include soil, wind, water, oxygen availability, and humidity.

4. Answers will vary depending on students' experiments.

5. Answers will vary. Generally bare ecosystems are warmer than those with vegetation.

6. Answers will vary. Removing native vegetation, or replacing it with grass or crops, generally causes warming.

13. THE ROLE OF DECOMPOSERS IN THE NITROGEN CYCLE

Idea for class discussion: Ask students to list the elements in the four major macromolecules (carbohydrates, lipids, proteins, and nucleic acids) that plants need to grow. Have them explain the role of each macromolecule. Have students speculate on what could happen if some of the elements were not available.

Notes to the teacher: A month or two before the experiment, start a compost pile in which you have layered dead, shredded leaves with soil. Moisten the compost pile occasionally to support the growth of bacteria and the breakdown of the leaves. Alternately, visit an area where decayed leaves are part of the topsoil. Also collect some soil that does not contain decayed leaves.

Start corn or bean seedlings for the students. Plant seeds in peat pots about a week before the experiment. Plant enough seeds to provide each lab group with eight seedlings.

Analysis

1. Nitrogen is released from the tissues of dead plants and animals by decomposition.

2. Answers will vary according to student results.

3. A dead leaf still contains all of its nutrients. A decomposed leaf has undergone chemical changes that release nitrogen and other nutrients into the environment.

4. The variable is the addition of decayed leaves to the soil.

5. Answers will vary but could include time of day, temperature, and amount of water.

6. If all variables are not kept constant, one cannot interpret the results of the experiment.

14. INVASIVE SPECIES' IMPACT ON AN ECOSYSTEM

Idea for class discussion: Explain to students that if they were to visit another country, they could not bring in plants from that country back into the United States. Ask them why bringing foreign plants to the United States is a bad idea.

Analysis

1. Answers will vary depending on events in the simulation.

2. The populations were stable because of the predator-prey relationship.

3. Rabbits consumed a lot of the plants, keeping sheep from getting enough food.

4. Answers will vary but students will probably say no, there is not enough food.

5. Kudzu is an invasive species because it was introduced to a new environment and it does not have any natural predators. Kudzu out-competes some native plants for food and water. Because the vine grows fast, it can cover large areas of plants, preventing them from getting sunlight.

15. COMPONENTS OF AN ECOSYSTEM

Idea for class discussion: Ask students to suggest some methods the class might use to gather information about the components of a local ecosystem. Use their ideas as an introduction to the experiment.

Analysis

1. An ecosystem is a region in which a group of organisms interact with each other and the environment.

2. The Sun provides energy to ecosystems.

3. Answers will vary based on animal observed.

4. Answers will vary based on animal observed.

5. Answers will vary based on location observed.

6. Answers will vary but should include several types of plants and animals.

7. Answers will vary. Microscopic organisms are present all through an ecosystem. They have several roles including production of glucose and decomposition.

8. Answers will vary but could include: (a) organisms can only survive within a narrow range of temperatures; (b) organisms require oxygen; (c) organisms require water.

16. COMMUNITY SUCCESSION IN MILK

Idea for class discussion: Find out what students know about bacteria and their ubiquitous nature in our lives. Point out that bacteria can be found almost everywhere. Discuss the fact that most bacteria are harmless to humans.

Analysis

1. The pH dropped over time because the milk became more acidic as it aged.

2. Answers will vary. The milk changed because of the changing community of microorganisms living in it.

3. Answers will vary. The population of harmless bacteria increased.

4. Answers will vary. The species that appear in succession of the milk environment are predictable.

5. The milk environment becomes more acidic.

6. In milk, each species of microorganism that moves in causes changes to the environment that make it possible for other species to survive. In an abandoned field, each species of plant or animal that moves in changes the field, making it possible for other species to become established.

17. DAY-LENGTH ADAPTATIONS IN SEEDS

Idea for class discussion: Talk to students about planting time in your locale. Ask them to pretend to be farmers and suggest the best time to plant their crops.

Analysis

1. Answers will vary. Students might write that seeds germinate best when days are at least 8 hours long.

2. Answers will vary depending on experimental results.

3. Answers will vary. Variables include (but are not limited to) temperature, amount of water, amount of fertilizer, and location.

4. Answers will vary.

5. Answers will vary. Students might suggest heating some seeds and planting them, along with seeds that have not been heated that will serve as a control.

18. HOW EFFECTIVE IS MIMICRY?

Idea for class discussion: Have students list some predators and their prey. Ask students how these prey protect themselves from their predators.

Analysis

1. Answers will vary. *Mimicry* is an adaptation in which one organism resembles another organism that is toxic or dangerous.

2. Mimics are usually nonpoisonous. They rely on their resemblance to a poisonous organism to protect them.

3. The beans with red *X*s were the toxic prey.

4. Unmarked pinto beans are more numerous than marked beans.

5. Answers will vary. Mimicry protects organisms because predators have trouble distinguishing the mimics from the toxic animals they resemble.

19. IDENTIFYING THE BENTHOS COMMUNITY

Idea for class discussion: Ask students to suggest locations in a pond where animals live. Introduce the concept that some organisms live in the soil at the bottom of the pond.

Review the concept of insect metamorphosis.

Analysis

1. Answers will vary depending on location and time of year.

2. Answers will vary depending on location and time of year.

3. Answers will vary depending on location and time of year.

4. Loss of benthic invertebrates will disrupt the food chain. These animals eat "low" on the food chain, consuming producers. For this reason, their loss will affect all of the organisms above them on the food chain.

5. Answers will vary. Loss of species and changes in the populations suggest that pollutants have reduced the quality of the water.

20. WATER AFFECTS TEMPERATURES IN BIOMES

Idea for class discussion: Review the concept of relative humidity and discuss how relative humidity affects plants and animals.

Note to the teacher: Place the thermometers in the one-hole stoppers prior to the activity so these are already prepared for the students.

Analysis

1. The test tube of sand lost the most heat.

2. The test tube of sand represented the desert because the sand is very dry like the desert biome. The test tube of water represented the tropical rain forest because the rain forest is so humid.

3. Areas near water cool more slowly at night. Water holds heat and releases it slowly to the surrounding region.

4. Answers will vary but could include wind, mineral content of the soil, and availability of light.

5. Answers will vary. The difference in abiotic factors would have a serious impact on their survival. For example, a tropical rain forest frog could not survive the direct sunlight and high temperatures of the desert.

6. Answers will vary. Gravel cools more slowly than sand, but faster than water.

Glossary

abiotic nonliving, as of chemical or physical factors in the environment

adaptation characteristic due to natural selection that helps organisms survive in their environment

adenosine triphosphate (ATP) the primary energy-carrying molecule in living things

aerobic related to, or living in, oxygen

albedo the amount of sunlight reflected from a surface

algal blooms proliferation of algae in waterways, often due to the addition of fertilizers

alluvial related to alluvium, soil or sediment deposited by running water

ammonia compound made of hydrogen and nitrogen that is produced by the anaerobic decay of organic matter

anaerobic not related to, or living in, oxygen

annelid a member of the phylum Annelida, segmented worm

aposematic coloration warning coloration that advertises an animal's toxins or venom

aquatic succession predictable changes that occur in an aquatic community over time

autotroph organism that makes its own food

benthos organisms that live in and on the floor of the sea or a body of freshwater

biodiversity large number and range of species within an ecosystem

biome large, ecological community that has similar climate and characteristic plant and animal inhabitants

biomonitoring using the organisms to draw inferences about the health of an ecosystem

biotic of or related to living chemical or physical factors in the environment

camouflage type of concealing coloration or structure that enables an organism to blend in with the environment

canopy the uppermost layer of branches in a forest formed by the tops of the tallest trees

carbonic acid weak acid (H_2CO_3) formed from the combination of carbon dioxide and water

carnivore organism that consumes animals

casein primary protein found in milk and milk products

cellular respiration aerobic biochemical reaction in which glucose is converted into ATP

chlorophyll green pigment in plants that enable them to capture the Sun's energy and use it for photosynthesis

climate long-term weather pattern in a region

climax community mature, relatively stable plant community that forms through the process of succession

cover the plants in a region that grow over the ground

crepuscular   active at twilight or dawn when light is low

cryptic coloration   patterns or colors that help conceal an animal from its predators

curdle   to change from a liquid into a solid

decomposer   organism that breaks down complex compounds into simpler ones

denitrification   process in which bacteria change nitrate into nitrogen gas

detritus   dead, particulate organic matter

dormant   in a condition of inactivity, rest, or suspended animation

ecosystem   natural unit formed of a community of interacting organisms and their environment

ectotherm   animal whose body temperature varies with the environment; cold-blooded animal.

endotherm   animal whose body temperature is regulated by its metabolism; warm-blooded animal

epiphyte plant that grows on top of another plant and derives its nutrients and oxygen from the air

excrement   waste products of an animal's digestive system

food chain   feeding relationships in an ecosystem that show how energy is transferred from producers to consumers

food web   all of the overlapping food chains in an ecosystem

germinate   to sprout or produce roots and shoots

greenhouse gases   layer of carbon dioxide and other gases in the atmosphere that trap heat near the Earth's surface

gross primary production   the amount of photosynthesis carried out by plants

hemoglobin   protein in the blood that binds to oxygen

herbivore   animal that only eats plants

heterotroph   organism that is not capable of making its own food

humus   decomposed organic matter in soil

hydrogen bond   weak bond that forms between the slight, opposite charges on molecules

imbibition   the process in which a seed takes in water

indicator species   species that is highly susceptible to change in the quality of its environment

invasive species   species that is not native to an area and can out-compete resident organisms

invertebrate   any of a large group of organisms that do not have a backbone

ion   atom or molecule that is electrically charged

latitude distance in degrees north or south of the equator

legume   plant whose roots support nitrogen-fixing bacteria that increase levels of nitrogen in the soil

limiting factor   any factor, such as food, water, or light, that limits the growth of a population

macroinvertebrates   animals without backbones that are large enough to be seen without the aid of a microscope

marsh   grassy wetland that may serve as the transition zone between an aquatic and terrestrial regions

metabolism   the sum total of all biochemical reactions that take place in a living thing to maintain life

microhabitat   small, specialized habitat within a larger one

migrate   to move from one area to another, especially on a seasonal basis

mimic   organism that has evolved to look like another organism, the model

model   organism whose appearance has been copied by another organism, the mimic

net primary production   the amount of photosynthesis carried out by plants after the photosynthesis that supports cellular respiration has been subtracted

niche   the role of an organism in its community

nitrifying bacteria   microbes that change ammonia and other organic nitrogen compounds into nitrates

nocturnal   active during the night

omnivore   organism that consumes both plants and animals

opportunistic feeder   organism that can use almost any type of food and is tolerant of most environments

pasteurized milk   milk that has been exposed to heat to destroy dangerous bacteria

pheromone   chemical signal secreted by some organisms that triggers a response in other organisms of the same species

photoperiod physiological response of some organisms to the length of day or night

photosynthesis   biochemical process in which chlorophyll traps the Sun's energy and uses it to make glucose

pioneer species   the first organisms to move into a new area, such as a newly formed sand dune or an abandoned field

plankton   free-floating, small organisms, including algae, small animals, and protists, that can be found on the surface of freshwater and in marine environments

plumule   the part of a germinating seed that will develop into a shoot

polar   having a positive end and a negative end

population   group of the same kind of organisms living within a community

positive feedback system   process in which the presence of a signal or product causes the production of more of the signal or product

precipitation   the falling to Earth of water in any form, including rain, snow, sleet, and hail

primary succession   development of a biological community in an area that in the past was barren, such as new rock produced by volcanic lava

producer   organism that contains chlorophyll and can make its own food

radicle   part of the germinating seed that will develop into the root

relative humidity   ratio of the amount of water vapor in the air to the amount of water vapor the air could hold

saprophage   organism that eats dead organic matter

scavenger   animal that feeds on dead organisms

secondary succession   development of a biological community in an area that has been disturbed, such as a plowed field

sedentary   staying in one area; not moving

seed   an embryonic plant and its food held within a protective seed coat

seed coat   tough, protective layer on the outside of a seed

self-mimicry   coloration or arrangement of structures so some peripheral area of a prey animal resembles the head, distracting predators and increasing the organism's chances of surviving an attack

stomata   openings in leaves, generally on the underside, through which gases are exchanged with the atmosphere

substrate   the material that makes up the seafloor or the bottom of a body of freshwater

symbiotic   relating to a relationship in which organisms of different species live together

transpiration   the evaporation of water from the leaves of plants

trophic   relating to a feeding level in a food chain

urea   water-soluble molecule that is formed by the breakdown of protein and excreted in urine

weathering   the breaking down of rocks on Earth's surface by chemical or physical forces

Weighing boat   container used to hold liquids or solids so they can be weighed.

Internet Resources

The World Wide Web is an invaluable source of information for students, teachers, and parents. The following list is intended to help you get started exploring educational sites that relate to the book. This list is just a sample of the Web material that is available to you. All of these sites were accessible as of January 2010.

Educational Resources

Anthoni, J. Floor. "Soil: Dependence—How Society Depends On Soil," 2000. Available online. URL: http://www.seafriends.org.nz/enviro/soil/depend.htm. Accessed January 10, 2010. Anthoni's interesting Web page discusses humans in the food chain and contrasts the positions of vegetarians and meat eaters.

"Biomes of the World." Marietta College. Available online. URL: http://www.marietta.edu/~biol/biomes/biomes.htm. Accessed January 10, 2010. On this interactive Web page, you can click on a biome and make a virtual visit.

Bradley, David. "The Properties of Water." Watercourse. Available online. URL: http://www.waterconservators.org/prop.html. Accessed January 10, 2010. Bradley explains why water creates hydrogen bonds and how these bonds affect its chemical characteristics.

Earth Observatory. Available online. URL: http://earthobservatory.nasa.gov/GlobalMaps/view.php?d1=MOD17A2_M_PSN#. Accessed January 10, 2010. An interactive map of the world shows how net primary productivity changes over a period of nine years.

Ecology Global Network. Available online. URL: http://ecology.com/index.php. Accessed January 10, 2010. The Ecology Global Network's goal is to educate the public and to protect the natural world. Links on this Web site include "What's New @ Ecology Today," where current articles are posted.

Farabee, M. J. "Community and Ecosystems Dynamics," June 6, 2007. Available online. URL: http://www.emc.maricopa.edu/faculty/farabee/BIOBK/BioBookcommecosys.html. Accessed January 10, 2010. Farabee's article contains a detailed discussion that includes biomes and community succession.

Fitzpatrick, Benjamin M., Kim Shook, and Rueben Izally. "Frequency-Dependent Selection by Wild Birds Promotes Polymorphism in Model Salamanders," 2009. BMC Ecology. Available online. URL: http://www.biomedcentral.com/1472-6785/9/12. Accessed January 10, 2010. In this paper for the advanced student, researchers report on their findings that a striped form of salamander has no survival advantage over the more common, unstriped form.

Global Change 1: Physical Processes: "The Flow of Energy: Primary Production to Higher Trophic Levels," October 31, 2009. Regents of the University of Michigan. Available online. URL: http://www.globalchange.umich.edu/globalchange1/current/lectures/kling/energyflow/energyflow.html. Accessed January 10, 2010. This Web page provides an excellent explanation of how ecosystems obtain and use energy.

Harrison, John Author. "The Nitrogen Cycle. Of Microbes and Men," 2003. Vision Learning. Available online. URL: http://www.visionlearning.com/library/module_viewer.php?mid=98. Accessed January 10, 2010. Harrison explains how microbes convert nitrogen into nitrogen compounds that plants and animals can use.

Houghton, Richard. "Understanding the Global Carbon Cycle," 2007. Woods Hole Research Center. Available online. URL: http://www.whrc.org/carbon/index.htm. Accessed January 10, 2010. Houghton explains the role of carbon in the biosphere.

Massengale's Biology Junction. "Population Genetics and the Hardy-Weinberg Law." Available online. URL: http://www.biologyjunction.com/hardyweinberg_problems.htm. Accessed January 10, 2010. Massengale, a biology teacher, explains how the Hardy-Weinberg Law determines whether evolution has occurred in a population.

Pidwirny, Michael. "Introduction to the Biosphere," *Primary Productivity of Plants*, May 7, 2009. PhysicalGeography.net. Available online. URL: http://www.physicalgeography.net/fundamentals/chapter9.html. Accessed January 10, 2010. In this chapter of his ebook, Pidwirny differentiates between primary and gross productivity of plants.

"Predator Prey Interaction: Lecture Content." Available online. URL: http://www.tulane.edu/~ggentry/ECOL/Lex/Eco04Lect15.ppt. Accessed January 10, 2010. This excellent PowerPoint presentation from Tulane University includes photographs of animals showing warning coloration and camouflage coloration.

Science Daily. "Frog Fungus Hammering Biodiversity in Communities," September 23, 2009. Available online. URL: http://www.sciencedaily.com/releases/2009/09/090922160100.htm. Accessed January 10, 2010. This article reports on the damage caused by fungus to a frog population in Central America.

"Simpsons Diversity Index," 2004. Offwell Woodland and Wildlife Trust. Available online. URL: http://www.countrysideinfo.co.uk/soil.htm. Accessed January 10, 2010. The Simpson's Diversity Index is a method of quantifying the biodiversity of a region.

Soil Ecology and Management, 2004. Michigan State University. Available online. URL: http://www.safs.msu.edu/soilecology/soilecology.htm. Accessed January 10, 2010. This Web page discusses the biotic and abiotic factors of soil.

Starbuck, Christopher J. "Making and Using Compost," April 2001. Department of Horticulture, University of Missouri Extension. Available online. URL: http://extension. missouri.edu/publications/DisplayPub.aspx?P=G6956. Accessed January 10, 2010. Starbuck explains how microorganisms break down material to form compost and succession in the compost community.

Stewart, Robert. "Marine Fisheries Food Web," August 3, 2009. Our Ocean Planet. Available online. URL: http://oceanworld.tamu.edu/resources/oceanography-book/ marinefoodwebs.htm. Accessed January 10, 2010. Steward explains how terrestrial and ocean food webs differ. His Web page also has a link to a discussion of microbial food webs.

U.S. Environmental Protection Agency. Available online. URL: http://www.epa.gov/. Accessed January 10, 2010. The EPA Web site has links to information and data on the environment.

Watson, David E. "Photosynthesis Is For The Birds—And Everything Else," 2009. F.T. Exploring Science and Technology. Available online. URL: http://www.ftexploring. com/photosyn/photosynth.html. Accessed January 10, 2010. Watson discusses and illustrates the roles of autotrophs and the chemical process of photosynthesis.

Periodic Table of Elements

Key:
```
 1  ── atomic number
 H  ── symbol
1.008 ── atomic weight
```

Numbers in parentheses are the atomic mass numbers of radioactive isotopes.

1	2	3	4	5	6	7	8	9	10	11	12	13	14	15	16	17	18
1 H 1.008																	2 He 4.003
3 Li 6.941	4 Be 9.012											5 B 10.81	6 C 12.01	7 N 14.01	8 O 16.00	9 F 19.00	10 Ne 20.18
11 Na 22.99	12 Mg 24.31											13 Al 26.98	14 Si 28.09	15 P 30.97	16 S 32.07	17 Cl 35.45	18 Ar 39.95
19 K 39.10	20 Ca 40.08	21 Sc 44.96	22 Ti 47.88	23 V 50.94	24 Cr 52.00	25 Mn 54.94	26 Fe 55.85	27 Co 58.93	28 Ni 58.69	29 Cu 63.55	30 Zn 65.39	31 Ga 69.72	32 Ge 72.59	33 As 74.92	34 Se 78.96	35 Br 79.90	36 Kr 83.80
37 Rb 85.47	38 Sr 87.62	39 Y 88.91	40 Zr 91.22	41 Nb 92.91	42 Mo 95.94	43 Tc (98)	44 Ru 101.1	45 Rh 102.9	46 Pd 106.4	47 Ag 107.9	48 Cd 112.4	49 In 114.8	50 Sn 118.7	51 Sb 121.8	52 Te 127.6	53 I 126.9	54 Xe 131.3
55 Cs 132.9	56 Ba 137.3	57-71*	72 Hf 178.5	73 Ta 180.9	74 W 183.9	75 Re 186.2	76 Os 190.2	77 Ir 192.2	78 Pt 195.1	79 Au 197.0	80 Hg 200.6	81 Tl 204.4	82 Pb 207.2	83 Bi 209.0	84 Po (210)	85 At (210)	86 Rn (222)
87 Fr (223)	88 Ra (226)	89-103‡	104 Rf (261)	105 Db (262)	106 Sg (263)	107 Bh (262)	108 Hs (265)	109 Mt (266)	110 Ds (271)	111 Rg (272)	112 Uub (285)		114 Uuq (285)		116 Uuh (292)		118 Uuo (?)

*lanthanide series

57 La 138.9	58 Ce 140.1	59 Pr 140.9	60 Nd 144.2	61 Pm (145)	62 Sm 150.4	63 Eu 152.0	64 Gd 157.3	65 Tb 158.9	66 Dy 162.5	67 Ho 164.9	68 Er 167.3	69 Tm 168.9	70 Yb 173.0	71 Lu 175.0

‡actinide series

89 Ac (227)	90 Th 232.0	91 Pa 231.0	92 U 238.0	93 Np (237)	94 Pu (244)	95 Am (243)	96 Cm (247)	97 Bk (247)	98 Cf (251)	99 Es (252)	100 Fm (257)	101 Md (258)	102 No (259)	103 Lr (260)

Index